FRED
TITMUS

FRED TITMUS

MY LIFE IN CRICKET

FRED TITMUS
WITH
STAFFORD HILDRED

Published by John Blake Publishing Ltd,
3, Bramber Court, 2 Bramber Road,
London W14 9PB, England

www.blake.co.uk

First published in hardback in 2005

ISBN 1 84454 124 X

British Library Cataloguing-in-Publication Data:

A catalogue record for this book is available from the British Library.

Design by www.envydesign.co.uk

Printed in Great Britain by CPD, Wales

1 3 5 7 9 10 8 6 4 2

Papers used by John Blake Publishing are natural, recyclable products made
from wood grown in sustainable forests. The manufacturing processes
conform to the environmental regulations of the country of origin.

Every attempt has been made to contact the relevant copyright-holders,
but some were unobtainable. We would be grateful if the appropriate people
could contact us.

To my wife Stephanie.

ACKNOWLEDGEMENTS

The game of cricket has introduced me to many wonderful characters and I would like to thank all of them for helping to make my time so enjoyable. But I would particularly like to thank John Murray and Peter Parfitt, two old team-mates who have become lifelong friends, who both helped greatly with the preparation of this book.

Thanks to John Blake Publishing. Above all, thanks to James Ravenscroft, a most talented editor, who recently passed away. His patience, kindness and conscientiousness will always be remembered.

CONTENTS

INTRODUCTION

Meeting your childhood heroes can be a dangerous experience. Those precious early images can disappear in a moment and you can never quite regain them. As a newspaperman, it can happen to you at any time. Dispatched on one of my earliest Fleet Street missions to interview Manchester United's finest player, who was one of my early icons, I learned that sometimes it is better never to encounter inspirational figures face to face. Certainly, the sight of the footballing genius George Best lying flat out drunk in a Fulham pub will live with me for ever. He was still dribbling, but not in the way that used to inspire thousands of delirious fans to leap for joy. Happily on the plus side, I've also experienced three good reasons for believing that the real thing can live up to your youthful imagination.

In 1982, on a visit to California with our ten-month-old daughter Claire, my wife Janet and I were astonished when Muhammad Ali wandered out of a restaurant in front of us. Confronted by arguably the greatest boxer who ever lived, who also just happened at the time to be the best-known guy on the planet, I searched for something suitable to say. Sadly, I came up with a rushed and garbled, 'CanIhaveyourautographplease?' As I was clutching a camera, the former world champion suggested a picture of him holding the baby. Click... and the moment was over.

My wife was much more impressed by John Travolta, who turned out to be the great man's lunch partner, but Muhammad, I am happy to record, was polite, charming and every bit the regular hero.

Another boyhood favourite I once met was Jimmy Greaves. Don't listen to descriptions of Wayne Rooney or Thierry Henry as the greatest goalscorers who ever played. They are pale imitations of the genuine article. Sixties soccer star Jimmy Greaves really was the greatest. He was quick, cocky and clinically efficient. Years after he had finished with the game and won his painful public battle with alcohol, Jimmy arrived in Birmingham in his new role as a TV pundit and, as the local showbusiness hack on the city's evening paper, I was sent to interview him.

Chatting to actors and actresses had never raised a flicker of nervousness. I even once went up in a small lift with Sophia Loren and remained able to conduct an almost coherent conversation. But the prospect of meeting Jimmy Greaves in the flesh reduced me to a jibbering wreck with the interviewing technique of a goldfish. Happily, Jimmy was gloriously funny and down to earth. We spoke in the office of the great Billy Wright, then head of ATV Sport, who had a drinks cabinet the size of Molineux. Anxious to deal with the controversial question of his alcoholism head on, Jimmy grinned and observed laconically, 'Between you and me, I think I'm the only guy in the sports department without a drink problem.'

But in the summer times of my youth, when the sun seemed to shine for months on end, the cricketer Fred Titmus was my childhood inspiration. There was something about the way the Middlesex and England all-rounder conducted himself on the cricket field that did it for me. My friends drooled about the elegant stroke play of Denis Compton or Ted Dexter, or the pace of Freddie Trueman or Brian Statham, but Fred Titmus was always my cricketing hero. Fred could do anything – bat, bowl or field – and he always seemed to be able to produce a really great performance when it was really needed. He wasn't flashy or colourful, but if you wanted someone to dig you out of a hole when things were going badly, then Fred always seemed the man to turn to. Unless they were talking about cameras, people didn't tend to use words like 'focussed' back in the 1950s or 1960s, but I suppose that's what he was. He was always alert, always concentrating and yet a smile never seemed to be far from his lips. To a shy, sports-mad schoolboy from the sticks of Lincolnshire, Fred always seemed like the great professional.

So when the German estate agent on the Mediterranean island of Majorca happened to mention that one apartment on the complex we were looking at had already been sold to an Englishman called Titmus, my ears pricked up like Red Rum's at the approach of the finishing line. 'Not *Fred* Titmus, by any chance?' I asked nervously, with images of sunshine and flashing willow in my mind.

'Yes,' said Tanya. 'In England, he was a cricket player.'

After that, the tiny flat we were considering suddenly seemed surprisingly spacious. The dodgy plumbing was no longer a problem and the view became instantly breath-taking. And two years ago, Fred Titmus and I became neighbours.

When we first met by the pool, I blurted out that the last time I had seen him in the flesh had been at The Oval in 1964 on the memorable day when Freddie Trueman took his 300th Test wicket. Fred instantly recalled the moment. 'Yes,' he smiled. 'Colin Cowdrey took the catch and I ran from mid-off to make sure I was the first to congratulate Fred.' Then he added with a twinkle, 'I knew Freddie was going to hit the headlines and I wanted to make sure I would be on all the pictures.'

That was the first of many marvellous moments I have been lucky enough to share with the Middlesex maestro. We were pushed together partly because, with the exception of a solitary Spanish family and a Norwegian couple, all of the other 73 owners on our complex were German. They were mostly icily polite on every occasion but, unknown to Mr Titmus and myself, they were also locked in a bizarre and bitter battle for control of the community we had just bought into. Some of the owners had a firm and unshakeable conviction that it was a good thing to spend community money as if we had all just won the Euro Lottery. Painters arrived from Germany and stayed at our expense in the best hotels while they slowly worked their way round the building. Expensive guttering was erected on Majorcan buildings designed to allow rainwater to run freely away without assistance.

And then Fred Titmus was accused of stealing the sun-loungers from the Germans. This was not just a potential front page lead for the *Daily Mail*, but an unpleasant real-life slur. Fred's lovely wife Stephanie had innocently purchased sun-loungers for their garden which were similar to the ones provided round the pool for the community. The president, with all the tact and diplomacy of a Panzer division, started enquiring if Mr and Mrs Titmus were aware that the sun-loungers were to be left round the pool and not to be taken into individual gardens. Even when Stephanie quietly showed the invoice and explained the coincidence, no-one the grace to apologise.

The next event was the community's annual general meeting which went on for an astonishing 12 hours as two groups of angry Germans hurled what sounded like very unpleasant insults at each other. Fred and I were stunned by the intensity of the arguments. Our wives tried hard to understand why these largely elderly Germans were so upset by each other. Evidently, the controlling group were being opposed by a growing company of fellow owners who did not wish to spend money like crazed millionaires. Fred listened for a while and then whispered to me, 'No wonder this lot lost the war,' and we decided to adjourn to a nearby watering hole.

There, as I began to draw from Fred some happy memories of a wonderful cricketing career, the idea for this book sprang up. We adjourned to our favourite hostelry, La Musica in Cala Bona, where the owner, a fine tenor called Joaquin Garcia entertains his customers with operatic arias, while his hard-working wife Jackie acts as social secretary for what appears to be the entire island. In these welcoming surroundings, I sat and listened to my hero talk modestly and humorously about his extraordinary career. I thought I knew all about Fred's cricketing days but, as he reminisced about the fun and the characters of a sporting life that went on as a player over five decades and as an England selector long after that, I realised I knew almost nothing.

Fred is one of only five cricketers to have taken more than 2,500 wickets and scored more than 20,000 runs. But he would much rather talk about Shirley Bassey being ordered out of the England dressing room, than the day he bowled out the great Len Hutton when he was only 17 years old.

Meeting your hero *can* be a hugely enjoyable experience. I hope this book is half as much fun to read as it was to write.

Stafford Hildred, April 2005

1

PLAYING WITH THE
BIG BOYS

My cricketing career got off to a surprisingly good start, and all because I was angry. As a 16-year-old ground staff boy at Lord's, I was fully prepared for several years selling scorecards and sweeping out stands before I got the chance to make my name for Middlesex. But one of the perks of the job was a session or two in the nets every week to polish up your skills. The trouble was that I'd missed out on my turn with the bat for three or four weeks and I was definitely not happy. I thought 'Blow this', and I was having a moan to anyone who would listen that I was not getting any practice in.

Eventually, my chance came and I got a net. But it takes time to calm down and I was still so angry that I went in determined to knock the ball not just out of the ground but preferably out of St John's Wood as well, if possible. I went bang ... bang ... bang ... and I seemed to have my eye in and I hit the ball all over the place as hard as I could.

To my immense good fortune, this outrageous and immature display of teenage petulance coincided exactly with the arrival at the nets of the Middlesex chief coach Archie Fowler in the company of the county stalwarts RWV (Walter) Robins and GO (Gubby) Allen. They were involved in a sudden and urgent search for a player to reinforce the team, weakened by injuries and Test calls, that was due to play Somerset at Bath at the weekend.

'That's the boy,' said captain Robins and pointed at me. He came across and said, 'How would you like to play for your county?'

I was so astonished by the attention and the remarkable question that I could only reply, 'Very much, sir.' I was suddenly worried. I knew my cricket gear was mainly in the wash at home and the shops were closed by then. But, in the changing room, my fellow ground staff boys were quick to rally round and lend me boots and flannels and all that I needed. Archie Fowler was more amazed at the selection than the clothes hunt. Generously, he said, 'This has never happened before in my experience, and I've been in the game for 39 years. I think I'm as proud as the boy himself. He won't let this go to his head.'

Strangely, I did not feel frightened or overawed by the challenge. This was June 1949 and I had only arrived at Lord's at the start of the season. I didn't know anyone in the team. I had bowled at Gubby Allen in the nets and that was my total experience of meeting the county players.

I went home and said, 'I've got to go to Bath tomorrow, Dad. I am playing for Middlesex.'

'Don't be so bloody silly,' he replied.

I had to work hard to convince him, and then, of course, he was very proud. He had been a keen sportsman in his youth. He was a boxer but he had very poor eyesight which always got in the way of his own chance of sporting success.

I should have been selling scorecards at the Test match at Lord's between England and New Zealand, but instead I went down to Bath on the 7.20am train from Paddington which was a daunting experience in itself. The rest of the team were already in the West Country as they'd just had a match against Gloucestershire. I met most of my new team-mates for the first time on the morning of the match. I didn't know any of them but they all tried hard to put me at my ease and insisted that it was just another game of cricket and I'd already played quite a few of them. I went in at number nine and scored 13 runs and I was pleased to hit three fours. I bowled a couple of overs and got four not out in the second innings. Afterwards, both Walter Robins and Gubby Allen congratulated me and I slowly started to realise that I was a county cricketer. Walter Robins even told a newspaper that I was a born cricketer who might one day play for England. My mum and dad were very proud. With hindsight, the last-minute call was the perfect way to start. I didn't have time to be nervous.

It was only a couple of miles or so from my home in London's Kentish Town to Lord's, but it was a journey I had dreamed of making for years as a sports-mad schoolboy. My earliest hero was Denis Compton, although that was more for his feats as a footballer for the Arsenal. Denis was a very talented left-winger, whom Joe Mercer reckoned was the most gifted footballer he had ever played with. I had a friend called Billy Smallwood who lived in the block of flats with me and he asked me to come with him to Lord's to watch cricket. At that age – perhaps 13 or 14 – I was more interested in playing than watching, so I was not too keen. But Billy was persistent. He said Denis Compton was playing.

I said, 'What? The outside left? Does he play cricket as well?'

Billy assured me that he did, and we went. He had been going through a rare bad patch, but the day Billy and I went he was back in the team and back to scintillating form. He scored a century and I was hooked on cricket from that day onwards. Denis Compton made it look so glamorous and exciting. I loved it. From that moment, he became God! When I discovered Denis Compton also played cricket for Middlesex, I set my sights on getting to Lord's.

According to all the records, including the respected *Wisden*, I was born in Kentish Town. But, in fact, the third happy event in the Titmus family, when I followed my brother and sister into the world, occurred in Somers

Town, just by King's Cross Station, on 24 November 1932. We moved to Kenbrook House, Leighton Road in Kentish Town in 1938. Some of my earliest cricket was played on Parliament Hill Fields at the bottom of Hampstead Heath, which was the nearest piece of green belt to my home. My friend Denis Marden, who had a bat, and I used to go there together and take turns to thrash out impressive innings.

I attended Burghley Road School at Tufnell Park where my strongest memories are of long rambling games of football and cricket which were occasionally rudely interrupted by lessons. We also went to Mr Snow's Play Centre where that excellent teacher coached us dutifully in both great sports.

I was eight in 1939, and my sister Peggy was ten, when we were evacuated to Rutland. Peggy could have been a runner, but she never took it up seriously. We were the last two kids to be picked because we wanted to stay together. I was never worried because I had my big sister to look after me. Being in the middle of the country, we stayed with Mr Wood the policeman and his wife and daughter, who were very very nice people. But having come from London, it did seem a bit quiet. The only benefit I gained, really, was years later when we started going away to play cricket, and by that time I was not bothered about living away from home.

Later, I was evacuated to Leicester, and at the school there was a teacher called Mrs Gardener who was also very keen on cricket. She had us playing cricket and football and she was a very good coach at both sports. The old boy I was staying with was a lay preacher. They were a wonderful family who encouraged any interest in sport, which was fine by me. I made friends with a boy called Maurice Hallam, who went on to captain Leicestershire at cricket and to play for Leicester City at football. We were good friends as schoolboys as he lived in the next road, but we lost touch when I moved back to London. Years later, when Middlesex played Leicestershire, I saw the name Maurice Hallam on the team sheet and I went into their dressing room to see if it was the same person. I was greeted by a cry of 'Fred! I thought it would be you'. It was great to see him again and we renewed our friendship, which lasted for many years until his sad early death.

To this day, I hold a slight grievance towards Leicestershire because I wrote for a trial with a local boys' team and never received a reply. I wasn't there long, just while the buzz bombs were threatening London. I was up there when I got a message through that I had won a scholarship to William Ellis Grammar School. That came as an expensive surprise to my mother and father. Knowing I was not exactly a genius in the classroom, they had said, 'If you pass the exam, you can have a brand-new bicycle.' It can't have been easy for them, but they did stump up and buy me a bike. I was just as shocked as they were at my success.

We lived in a block of council flats called Kenbrook House. That's where I learned my cricket and football, because we had a good playground. We used to play for hours and, occasionally, the old janitor would come out and kick us off. We would just wait a while and then go back and start playing again. My mother was a cook in the war at a local school and my dad was on the railway. Sadly, he wasn't a well man and a number of times I had to go down on a Friday to pick his money up. He was ill and he had desperately poor eyesight. I could walk past him in the road without being recognised if I didn't speak up.

My dad was very much a sports person but he was nearly blind and couldn't actually see me play. Years later, when I played against Australia, all the parents were invited and he came with my mother. But he couldn't see the wicket. He came and she talked him through what was going on and he was very moved by it. Unfortunately, it rained for half the day anyway. He used to sit only a few inches from the television, his eyes were so bad.

I was always keen on sport but, at first, I was a keen boxer at school and even became junior heavyweight champion. I went to St Pancras Boxing Club as well, but when I got in the ring with the trainer I realised it was not for me. I would have weighed in at about 11 stone then and the trainer was smaller and lighter than me by quite a bit. But he hit me on the chin and I thought, 'Ouch, that hurt.' He had been quite a good boxer in his time and I thought, 'If a little bloke like that can hit me that hard, then somebody my own size could really do some damage.' I decided cricket was much safer.

I dropped boxing, but we always had a punchbag at home. The more I played, the more I enjoyed cricket and I managed to get in the school first team when I was only 13.

I visited Lord's as a schoolboy to watch matches and I remember once when I went in the interval I saw some of the young ground staff boys in the nets at the back of the stand. I saw some boys bowling. They were only a little bit older than me and I can recall thinking that they didn't look any better than me.

I left school because, in spite of my previous astonishing exam success, I really couldn't see myself passing any more, so I wondered what the point was of staying on if I wasn't going to get the qualification. I left school at 16 and I became the telephone answerer and general gofer for a solicitors' office in London. I very soon discovered office work was not for me and, in any case, I wasn't training to be a solicitor, I was training to be a clerk

When I went back in for the school leaving day, the headmaster said, 'Titmus, I do hope you're not going to make sport a career and waste your education.'

'Oh, no, sir,' I lied quickly. 'Never.'

The next time I saw him, I was walking round at Lord's, having played for Middlesex. He came up to me and said, 'My dear boy. We're so proud of you at school.' I thought, 'Well, that wasn't quite what you said to me six months ago.'

I thought I could do as well as the ground staff lads I'd seen and that gave me the confidence to apply to Lord's myself. That earned me the chance of a trial, and I ended up bowling in a net behind the ladies' refreshment room to Denis Baldry, later a Middlesex colleague, and Tony Catt, who went on to play for Kent. I bowled only six balls and I was not invited to bat.

Bill Watkins, who had been on the previous Australian tour as scorer, and Ronnie Aird, who was a past secretary of the MCC, watched me. 'You'll do,' said Bill… and I was in. I was shocked and delighted. A couple of weeks later, I got a letter formally inviting me to join the staff. So I quickly gave up my legal career as general dogsbody.

An astonishing volume of publicity followed my youthful début; it was suggested in some papers that I had been brought up in grinding poverty, which was never the truth. My mother and father both worked hard. We lived in a block of council flats, certainly, but I never felt we were poor and neither were our neighbours, so far as I can remember. The scramble to get kitted out helped to lead to the wrong impression. It was 'poor little Fred from the buildings who hasn't got a shirt'. I had shirts all right and I had flannels, but I was only 16 and I hadn't got a wardrobe full of them. My best cricket gear was in the wash being cleaned for a weekend game. My older stuff was not smart enough for a county match and that was why I had to borrow a few things. The Press wrote up the incident so that it looked as if the Titmus family were living in a slum. It was an interesting early lesson that newspapers never like to let the facts get in the way of a good story.

More embarrassing were some of the headlines which suggested I was 'THE BEST DISCOVERY SINCE COMPTON'. Some bright journalist with columns to fill had compared my first game for Middlesex with the début of Denis back in 1936. Evidently, he had also been watched in the nets by Robins and Allen and we had both gone on to share in stands with Allen. Denis scored 14 against my 13, but it was still a pretty thin and tenuous link. I played just that one county game that year while Denis Compton, who was 18 years old at the time, stayed in the side until the end of the season and scored more than 1,000 runs. Denis was my hero as a boy and, to this day, I've never seen a more exciting player. Anyone who's seen Compton bat knows that there is nobody else quite like him.

I just loved playing cricket. I had scored quite a few runs for the Cross Arrows, the Lord's junior side. I even managed a couple of centuries and an average of 93. Cross Arrows was a side made up of Middlesex players and boys from the MCC staff. Walter Robins was captain that year and he selected me to play about a dozen times. He was an inspirational leader and I was always determined to reach any run target he gave us.

It was a wonderful first season. At the club's annual dinner, I was presented with an inscribed bat. I was also ordered by no less than Sir Pelham Warner (former England and Middlesex captain) to get my hair cut. He suggested I looked more like a poet than a cricketer and photographs of the time do show that I had quite an unruly head of hair. It was a glorious time in my life. As I cycled home to Kentish Town, I sometimes had to pinch myself that this was all really happening to me.

It was such a fairytale beginning that I don't think I ever quite shook off the 'little boy lost' image. I was never the tallest player in the game but, then again, I was not the shortest either. In fact, I'm 5 foot 9 inches, but my youth at the time of my début projected such a strong image of me as a boy among men that I never did quite throw off the 'gallant little Fred' descriptions that have lasted a lifetime. I think people like their heroes either 10 foot tall or 5 foot nothing, and I know which category I've been slotted into. Sometimes, I think that the better I played, the smaller I became.

But it wasn't quite all cricket in those wonderful youthful days when the sun seemed to shine all day long and we always felt as though we had energy to burn. At school, we used to play soccer under a Mr Snow, who had obviously been a very good footballer. He was well thought of at Chelsea where he got me a trial with the youth team and I went down there and played a number of games for Chelsea's nursery team, Tudor Rose. Later, I moved to Watford where the manager was Eddie Hapgood, who offered to take me on as an apprentice, but I fell over in a game and did a cartilage. That virtually ended my footballing career.

Perhaps one of the most memorable moments of those early Watford days was meeting another of my heroes, the great Tom Finney, even if my humble task was simply to serve him tea at half-time. Many years later, I met him again at an FA Cup Final eve at Wembley and was thrilled that he actually remembered the particular match and the score… though not the tea boy!

Lord's was an imposing place for an unsophisticated 16-year-old to enter back in those strangely euphoric post-war days of 1949. Rationing might have been the order of the day but there was a real optimism in the air. The last game I played in that season was for Denis Compton's Benefit XI at Hayes. It was Denis's benefit year and, before the match, he smiled and told me that he would return the favour and play for me in my benefit year. I walked home afterwards as if I was walking on air.

2

CAREER OPENER

After my early introduction to the Middlesex side, I was heartened about my chances of making it as a county cricketer, but I was well aware that I still had an awful lot to learn. So I was delighted when I was dispatched after the 1949 season to Alf Gover's cricket school in Wandsworth. Initially, I was sent to develop my seam bowling rather than off-spin! I think there had been some sort of breakdown in communication but, in fact, it did me a great deal of good. Alf taught me that the one great asset for any bowler, quick or slow, was to reach as high as he could when he got to the crease and bowl from as high an action as possible.

As the 1950 cricket season got under way, I discovered to my delight that my ground staff days were virtually over. I had never spent too much time bowling at members in the nets and I had done a very small amount of the dreaded scorecard selling. On the strength of my runs for the Cross Arrows, I was picked to play for the MCC against Surrey in early May and I was astonished to find myself on that first morning taking the field with Freddy Brown, Bill Edrich, Jack Robertson, Gilbert Parkhouse and other established players. It was my first big game at Lord's. I was only 17 and I simply could not bring myself to believe what was happening to me.

I came from a very ordinary working-class background but I never felt overawed by this remarkable traditional institution or any of its wealthier occupants. I went to a good grammar school, William Ellis, which helped to give me some confidence and the ability to mix with people from all walks of life. I was never aware of any snobbery. There were simply two different kinds of cricketers – amateurs and professionals. Their names were represented differently on scorecards. Amateurs were styled 'Mr' or 'Esq', or with their initials before rather than after their surnames. My professional status was spelt out in no uncertain terms in that next first game at Lord's.

It was a fine Saturday with a large crowd who were treated to an announcement over the loudspeaker, 'Ladies and Gentlemen, a correction to your scorecards… For "FJ Titmus", please read "Titmus FJ".'

I never really minded. I didn't want to change an antiquated system. I was proud to be a professional cricketer. I was more concerned with coming to terms with what was happening to me. Years later, Bill Edrich told me of the occasion when the MCC team arrived in Australia in 1954. On the first morning at Perth, he came down to breakfast and found himself sitting opposite newly selected Keith Andrew. He was 24 at the time and he was there as reserve wicket-keeper to Godfrey Evans. Keith just couldn't believe his luck. He looked at Bill wide-eyed and said, 'Is it true? Am I really in Australia?' I know just how he felt.

I have always been relieved that I was not on the borderline of getting chosen. We used to have boys come for trials and some were good enough and some weren't, but it is heart-breaking if your dreams are shattered, particularly when you're young. You feel so sorry for them. To go on and become a regular, you are lucky because the game becomes a way of life. I am lucky that I have never suffered from nerves. Right from the start, I took the view that if I have been picked for this side, then I must be good enough to play in it.

I didn't get to bowl in the first innings against Surrey, which was no great surprise to me. I was in the side for my batting and I went in at number five and scored a fairly nervous 10 before I was bowled by Jim Laker. In the second innings, I got three and, when the other side went in again, I did bowl a few overs. Mind you, half the side were thrown the ball in fairly desperate attempts to break a big stand between Constable and Parker. It was a pretty undistinguished Lord's début by any standards, but it was not held against me.

The following Saturday, I was selected to play for Middlesex against Hampshire and I bowled a chap called Rogers to take my first wicket in first-class cricket. It was a fabulous moment and I managed to stay in the side for most of the rest of the season.

I was very fortunate to be starting my career with Middlesex at a time of great change. Many of the senior players had been with the county since before the war and were coming to the end of their time. There was tremendous expectation at Lord's because this was the home of Denis Compton, Bill Edrich, Jack Robertson and Sid Brown. Together, they had scored a fantastic 12,000 runs in the glorious season of 1947 as Middlesex swept to the County Championship title. My hero Compton had scored 3,816 runs at an average of 90.85 in a season studded with no fewer than 18 centuries. Middlesex dipped to third in 1948 as Test calls seriously weakened the team at crucial points, but shared the title with Yorkshire in 1949. This was a county used to winning and it was to prove a desperately hard act to follow.

Denis was always such a nice, ordinary bloke, but you wouldn't have wanted to pick a fight with him. Two guys tried to rob him one night when he left Lord's, but he let them think he had something valuable in the boot of his car. When they opened it, he grabbed a bat and gave one of them a whack and they both ran off. Denis was the sort of chap who could handle himself in any crisis, but he was so kind and generous. If you mentioned that you liked anything, he would immediately offer it to you. I've never known anyone like him. He certainly was a ladies' man. All over the world, they used to turn up to meet him.

Bill Edrich was his great friend and he was much more serious; they were always great mates. Bill was a hard worker with his cricket but with Denis it just flowed. The other Middlesex star who should have played for England a lot more was Jack Robertson.

I played in 25 matches in the first team in 1950 and managed to finish with a tally of 55 wickets. I was very proud and two other young bowlers, 16-year-old Don Bennett and 17-year-old Alan Moss also joined that year. We were to see quite a lot of each other over the next few years. *Wisden* summed up the Middlesex situation kindly: 'Titmus (17) and Bennett (16) showed skill for their ages but those who watched the side were left in no doubt that Middlesex were going through a transitional period which may spread over some years before they rise again.'

We finished an undistinguished fourteenth in the table that year. I got 390 runs in my first full season to go with my wickets. I don't believe a good cricketer should ever feel too satisfied with himself or else complacency sets in, but I didn't feel I had done too badly. By the time September came, I had recorded my first first-class 50, against Somerset at Lord's, and had the thrill of having no less than Cyril Washbrook caught behind the stumps. This coup came when I opened the bowling with my medium-paced seamers.

In those days, I alternated between seamers and off-spinners and, I have to admit, that I was not always as accurate as I should have been. I bowled one very curious over to the Worcestershire skipper Ronnie Bird which included two wides, two no-balls and a purler of a ball that bowled the poor chap. He was completely confused by then and who could blame him? He just didn't know what to expect and, I have to confess that, that day, neither did I. I even managed to bowl the great Sir Len Hutton out, which was quite a coup. Afterwards, the master batsman said, 'How do you make the ball go like that, son?'

I didn't understand what he was talking about. I had just bowled trying to keep to a length. It was just a natural thing getting the ball to spin. I think it was because of all my practice with a tennis ball. It's all in the fingers and wrist, but it took me a long time realise what Len Hutton was asking about. To be honest, at the time I was not sure what I had done, so I did not know what to say and hesitated for a moment.

He took the pause for a wily reluctance to reveal my secrets and said, 'Ah, you're not going to tell me, are you? Quite right, lad, quite right.'

I soon learned more about my bowling and what I became known for – bowling off-breaks with an outswing that came back.

I was in the side primarily as a batsman and, in the Lord's match against Essex, I shared in a stand of 79 for the eighth wicket with Jim Sims. He was the oldest member of the side and I was the youngest. I will always be grateful that I played throughout that one full season with a senior professional like Jim, because he was not only a fine bowler, and a useful batsman, but he was also very definitely one of the great characters of the game.

Jim had a wonderfully droll sense of humour. The following season, when we played away to Somerset, we found their captain, SS Rogers, arriving at the wicket in the second innings 'on a pair' – that is, with the potential for being out first ball in two consecutive innings. John Warr had got him out without troubling the scorer in the first innings, and now Jim was bowling. 'You're all right, skipper,' said Jim as Rogers nervously passed him on the way to the wicket. 'I'll see you get off the mark.' He then bowled his googly, which the batsman totally failed to read and was bowled. As the hapless Mr Rogers passed him on the way back, Jim muttered quietly, 'Sorry, skipper, it slipped.'

Jim was one of the great characters of cricket, the people who bring the great game to life, in my view. It's perhaps an indication of the changing times that he was once pinched for parking near Selfridges and effortlessly talked himself out of a ticket. A policeman approached his car and said in the respectful words of those times, 'I've got to give you a ticket for this, sir. What is your name?'

'James Morten Sims, Lord's,' replied Jim.

'James Morten Sims, House of Lords?' asked the copper slightly more cautiously.

'No, no, no, not House of Lords… Lord's. *Lord's*!' said Jim, raising his voice.

'What's that mean, then?' asked the policeman.

'Lord's Cricket Ground, Marylebone,' said Jim.

'Where's that?' came the question.

'It's on your beat, man!' cried Jim in mock outrage. 'You mean to say you don't know it? Here, what's your number? I'm going to report you.'

Needless to say, Jim never did get pinched for parking that day.

I liked Jim a lot and learned a great deal from him, but we did not always get on perfectly. There was a bit of a patch at Trent Bridge I recall and I got a couple of wickets by bowling on to it. Jim fancied using this patch himself. Early on, Jim came sidling up to me and said, 'Tell the captain you want to bowl up at the other end.'

With the sublime confidence of youth, I said, 'I don't want to bowl at the other end. I want to bowl at this end.'

'Selfish little pup,' said Jim.

I confess I think I knew even then that you had to know how to stand up for yourself. I couldn't, in all honesty, disagree with Jim's description of me. I think in sport you have to be a little selfish if you really want to do well and succeed.

But we did not fall out for long. He made me laugh too much for that. He was having a rare off day and getting a lot of stick and someone smacked him towards the grandstand balcony where Alec Thompson was fielding.

The ball flew just above Alec's head for six. Jim turned to Don Bennett and asked where it had gone. 'Went over his head, Jim,' said Don.

'It should have hit him on top of the bloody head,' said Jim darkly.

Jim gave virtually his whole life to Middlesex. He played for a long time and later became the scorer and it was during a match against Kent at Canterbury years later that he had a heart-attack and died.

Senior Professional was an important position in a club. Sometimes, we would go away for a couple of weeks at a time because they would try to schedule the matches to reduce travelling wherever they could, so you might go to Old Trafford, say, and then on to Derbyshire for a match, before coming back to London. Only Compton, Edrich and Jack Robertson had motor cars. The rest of us had to go on the train, although the train service was quite good in those days. They did put us in first-class, specially if there was a diner, because by the time you'd finished the match it would be too late to get anything to eat before getting on the train. And it was the job of the twelfth man and the junior pro to get all the baggage; everyone else piled on the train and got stuck in.

They had three cabs waiting at the back door of the pavilion. The twelfth man and the junior pro were left to take care of all the great big cricket bags. You had to organise a couple of cabs for those and get porters to help you get it all on the train in time, handing out a tip here and a tip there. Eventually, you got to join the rest of the team who were all relaxing and enjoying a drink by then. Then, at the destination, they just got off and you had to get the bags off and organise porters again and find taxis and hand out another round of tips. It was hard work. 'Captain, don't worry about us, we'll get cabs.'

You would be away for ten days or two weeks and perhaps play three games in that time. So you spent quite a bit of money but, when you got back to Lord's, you had to claim your expenses. You would never take those expenses into the office yourself, you had to give them to Jim, the old senior pro, and he would pay you whatever you had claimed. He would add 50 per cent and take it into the office and keep the extra money for himself. You never questioned it. Jim was the king as far as the other pros were concerned. So when he told me to tell the captain that I wanted to bowl the other end, it was quite a thing for me to say, 'No, I don't want to bowl the other end.' But, as I said, you have to be able to stand up for yourself, in cricket and in life.

Jim received my instant respect because he had played for England four times in days when there were not nearly as many Test matches as there are today. He had toured Australia with Gubby Allen's team in 1936–7 and he was very near the end of his career in 1950.

Many of the other England players in the side were still in full cry. Jack Robertson got a lot of runs and Jack Young got a lot of wickets. Edrich and Compton did not have their best season but they had plenty of glory still to come. And Walter Robins was still there for ten matches, at least to lead the side. For a youngster like me, it was good company to be keeping. Mr Robins was a splendid captain who always succeeded in getting the best out of you in the field. He was always watching you and setting you an example. He made you feel keen and on edge all the time. He did not tolerate any slackness, whether you were the star player in the side or just the boy, as I was in those far-off days. If you allowed your standards to slip, you got the same going over whoever you were.

Walter Robins was an old die-hard amateur. I had immense respect for him. Once he caught me leaving the dressing room when the temperature was high in the 90s in London. He had a very high-pitched voice and he shouted, 'Fred.'

I turned back from the open door and looked at him.

'Where do you think you are going?'

'I'm going home, Mr Robins,' I said.

'Not dressed like that you're not. You put that jacket and tie on. You come in this ground properly dressed and you leave it properly dressed. Don't walk about without your coat on.'

I was 17 then and growing in confidence from having played, but Walter Robins soon cut me down to size. On the other hand, when he praised you it was praise indeed. When he said, 'Well done,' it meant something. For years, I valued his praise far more than I did most other people's, and not just because he became chairman of the Test Selection Committee. Like his contemporary, Stuart Surridge of Surrey, Walter Robins had the advantage of being a brilliant fielder. To be captain of a side and a bad fielder is to make life instantly difficult for yourself. There is an obvious lack of the good example which can affect the whole team. I don't mean that anyone consciously fields badly, because the captain occasionally puts one down, or lets one through, but if he does he is not well placed to complain when his men do the same. It can and does sometimes lead to a lowering of morale.

Sometimes, a captain who is a bad fielder can make up for his deficiencies by his general air of enthusiasm and alertness, but even so he is fighting an uphill battle if he has a clearly defined weakness in his game. As it happened, my introduction to top-class cricket came under a top-class skipper. The star team of the time needed star captaincy and that was exactly what it received.

Of course, I did not realise it then but I was sublimely fortunate to be playing my early cricket in such exalted company. Class ran through the whole side. One of my favourite players was the opener Jack Robertson who was a Test batsman of the highest quality who often seemed to receive a raw deal from the selectors. His record in the few Test matches he played in, and on the two tours he went on, proves this. Why he was overlooked so much is, to me, one of the mysteries of cricket; it shows that the old idea about Middlesex players getting more chances at international level because they play so much at Lord's is by no means true. But Jack's chances of selection were hardly helped because he was so often up against the established England opening pair of Cyril Washbrook and Len Hutton.

Jack was also a very fine fielder. He had such a reliable reputation that he brought the match to a standstill against Warwickshire at Edgbaston when he dropped an absolute sitter at mid-off. The whole team just stood open-mouthed in astonishment that he, of all people, had missed such an easy catch. 'Sorry, lads,' he said quietly. 'We all make mistakes sometimes.'

Jack's regular opening partner for Middlesex was Sid Brown, who reliably rattled up his 1,000 runs for the county every season. I believe Sid stood on his wicket more often than anyone I can remember because he played back to everything, but he was always looking for runs. Like many of the other players on that side, Sid was unfortunate to lose six vital seasons when the war interrupted play.

The two greatest players among my new colleagues were household names of the day, Bill Edrich and Denis Compton. Bill was a magnificent, fighting player who was well aware of his limitations. He did not have a great variety of shots at his disposal but he used the ones he possessed with tremendous verve and effectiveness. He was also full to the brim of the joys of life. As he said more than once, 'Some people like a party and some don't. I like a party.'

He was a relatively quiet chap on the field, by Middlesex standards at any rate, but at a party he would sing a song if you asked him. In fact, years later, on a famous occasion he and Denis Compton were visiting the cricketers of Ireland in Dublin as guests of honour. They had both indulged rather too heavily in generous amounts of liquid hospitality and were swaying gently in good company. Bill, though, had to deliver a speech at a formal dinner and those around him seriously doubted his capacity to make a great deal of sense. There was an air of growing alarm as Bill rose slowly to his feet and silence fell on the assembled gathering. He proceeded to sing 'Molly Malone' perfectly in tune and sat down again to tumultuous applause without ever troubling his audience with a speech. Bill was a great man.

His partner in run-getting was Denis Compton, who was, quite simply, larger than life. Denis was a law unto himself, a scatterbrained cricketing marvel who got away with murder on and off the field, not only because he had genius but also because he had such charm for anyone and everyone he encountered. Denis was just the same to the young lads crowding around the gate asking for autographs as he was to the chairman of selectors, which I've always taken as an indication of the true quality of the man. He would borrow your kit without asking, but he wouldn't mind if you borrowed his. Sometimes it could be annoying, as you would be looking for your bat because you were next in and you would look out into the middle and there would be Denis using it to great effect. But when you got out there with him, you didn't mind because he was an education to be with. His batting was out of this world and, although he built up a terrific reputation for being a player full of unorthodox attacking strokes, his defence, in fact, was absolutely sound.

Denis could play all games well and some outstandingly. His eye was so quick that he could take risks that ordinary players would be rash even to consider. And he was so full of life and energy. When he walked down the wicket to face a bowler in his great days he did not do it like any normal batsman. Sometimes he was out of his crease before the bowler had even started his run up. And even if he was on the wrong foot he was still good enough to play some sort of shot and most probably still get runs. Like most great batsmen, he had supreme confidence in himself and, on reflection, I am glad that I never had to bowl against him in any serious competition.

Of course, I often had to bat with him and that was a cricketing lesson in itself. You would seem him execute a stroke and, with the ball skidding away to the boundary, you would be thinking, 'You can't do that!'

One of the down sides of batting with Denis was that you would sometimes find yourself run out by him. He was a bad caller, and it's difficult to deny that, however much he was admired as a player. But even then, I always felt it was not entirely his fault. Because he was Denis and he called, you instinctively ran. If it had been someone else, you might well have weighed up the chances more carefully and shouted, 'No,' and ordered him back. But being Denis, you did as you were told and when there proved not to be a run in it, which somewhere in the darker recesses of your brain you had known all along, you sacrificed your wicket and not his.

Punctuality was never Denis's strong point. He appeared to have so much fun to fit into his life he occasionally arrived late for the day-to-day business of being the best batsman in the world. Often, he would present himself for play still in his dinner jacket from the night before with a tell-tale twinkle in his eye. Once he turned up an hour late at Lord's with the dramatic story that stones had been thrown at his car in Western Avenue. It couldn't have happened to anyone else.

On another occasion, we were at Worcester and he was known to be coming down from London on the morning of the match. When he had not appeared by 11.00am, we opened a book on his time of arrival, although none of us was unrealistic enough to bet on his arriving by the time the match started at 11.30am. The bets ranged in times from 11.35am–12.15pm, and the man with the latest time won. He was the nearest but, in fact, Denis ran on to the field 15 minutes after that. It was all treated as a joke. Somehow, this sort of eccentric behaviour was expected of Denis Compton and he had such a disarming manner about it all that we did not hold it against him. He was also no mean bowler, considering that he never really concentrated on that aspect of his game. He could be brilliant and he did once take 80 wickets in a season with his bewildering left-arm 'Chinamen', as we called them at the time, and googlies.

That first team I joined had Denis's older brother Leslie as wicket-keeper. Les was completely different in temperament to Denis but very kind and humorous just the same. As a batsman, Leslie was fairly cautious. I think he would have benefited greatly from showing a little more aggression, although I did not venture such an opinion at the time. Even so, the records show that he played many useful innings. One thing he was not good at, however, was playing off-spin. He used to play slightly too far forward and leave what we'd call a 'gate'. Jim Laker always reckoned that he was done out of four certain wickets a season when Leslie retired. I know I used to think that I wouldn't mind bowling at him.

The other main batsmen in the side were Harry Sharp and Alec Thompson. They were both very good county players who were unlucky to be there while Bill, Denis and Jack were in such fine form. They were usually the players to be dropped in August when the university players came into the side. The attack that season was usually opened by Laurie Gray, another player whose career was badly interrupted by the war. In his case, as a fast bowler, the lost years were more serious. Looking back now, he seems like an older edition of Alan Moss. Alan was not with us for many games in 1950 because he was serving in the RAF. He was a great county bowler who went on to play for England and never let the side down. He was just unfortunate, like all other fast bowlers of his generation, to be in his prime at the same time that Brian Statham and Freddie Trueman were in theirs. If he had been born a few years earlier or later, he would surely have played in a great many more Test matches.

Don Bennett suffered in the same way at county level, as Alan Moss and John Warr kept him out of the side for many matches early in his long career. Don was a remarkable athlete who could run 100 yards in 10.2 seconds, so he was able to cut off more than a few boundaries in his time. People used to say Don didn't have the height to become a fast bowler and, in those days, I used to think that this was all-important. In fact, it was one of the reasons I switched to concentrate on spin bowling. But my thoughts on the subject were radically changed years later when I met the great fast bowler Harold Larwood in Australia and was astonished to discover that he was shorter than my 5 foot 9 inches. This was another illusion shattered.

Jack Young took far more wickets for Middlesex than anyone else that summer and I learned a great deal from his advice and example. Some of his wise words took years to sink in and it was only many seasons later that I fully realised how much he knew about the game. But you have to listen when you're young because you never know when you might get a vital piece of information.

I had a difficult day at Cheltenham when I didn't take a wicket on a pitch that should by rights have helped me. I was a bit fed up and in the interval I turned to the old England batsman Charlie Barnett for advice. The wicket was turning but I couldn't seem to get anyone out and I couldn't understand why. Charlie said, 'Look, son, all good players play the turning ball well. What you've got to do is to get them to make a wrong movement before the ball turns. Don't let the ball go straight.'

I have mainly been very fortunate in avoiding injuries throughout my career but in that first full season I split a muscle in my right thigh playing against Warwickshire. It was very slow in mending and I missed playing against that year's tourists, the all-conquering West Indies side which won three of the four Tests against England.

At the end of the season, my 18th birthday was looming up and that meant call-up for National Service and what I imagined would be two years out of full-time cricket. But the situation was much better for me than for many other young players just starting to make their way in the game. At least I went off to fight the peace with one whole season's experience behind me and this was to stand me in very good stead. I couldn't really complain that the Royal Air Force authorities overlooked the fact that my main interest in life lay in playing cricket and had other duties lined up for me. If this was what King and country required, who was I to argue?

3

SERVING KING AND
COUNTRY

My time in the Royal Air Force began in exactly the same way as every other post-war national service-man... up to a point. I reported to the well-known reception centre at Padgate in Lancashire early in March 1951. After being kitted out and shouted at in that affectionate way the armed forces likes to use when welcoming new recruits, I was dispatched to Melksham, a small town near Trowbridge in Wiltshire, where I understood I was to commence two years of 'square-bashing'. It did not turn out quite like that, though. It was here that I began to be treated rather differently from the rest of my draft and to benefit greatly from my solitary season with Middlesex. A certain cricket-loving Air Vice-Marshall Sharp heard that I had been called up and wanted me to play for his side against the Army Staff College at Camberley.

It was not every day in the RAF of the early 1950s that a newly-recruited aircraftsman is rung up at his training camp by an Air Vice-Marshall. So when I was called to the flight office to take this call, I was treated with a mixture of guarded respect and thinly-disguised loathing. For all the flight officer knew, I could have been a personal friend of someone very important, so he had to be very careful as to how he stepped. I have to admit, having 'friends' in high places certainly did not make my life any harder.

Naturally, I agreed to play and when I arrived at the ground, I discovered I was far and away the lowest-ranking person in the side. Everyone else was commissioned and there were at least two Air Commodores in the side. I suppose once I had changed into my whites, anyone looking at the scorebook might have supposed that the initials A/C before my name also stood for that exalted rank, but having taken a look at my youthful self they would quickly have decided I was rather young to have attained such a rank.

Fortunately, I did quite well in the game and the Air Vice-Marshall was satisfied with my performance. He invited me to play for him again and told me to get in touch with him if ever I needed any help when I finished my training.

I had quite a lot of time off for cricket while serving in the RAF one way or another. I turned out quite a few times for Middlesex, as well as playing for the RAF and the Combined Services XI. For the RAF, I appeared at Lord's against the Navy and the Army, and at Worcester against the county side. The team included Jim Parks, Alan Moss, Ray Illingworth and David Heath, an opening batsman who played for Warwickshire.

At Portsmouth, I had my first experience of playing against a touring side. The South Africans were visiting that summer and the Combined Services XI lined up against them. Signalman Brian Close was in the team and he went on to dominate proceedings once the South Africans had declared on a formidable total of 499 for 5 wickets. Brian scored 66 and 135 not out. It was his first century in England. He was only 18 months older than me but he had already been on an Australian tour. That match was eventually drawn and we went on to play and lose to the Public Schools, Glamorgan, Warwickshire and Worcestershire. Alan Moss and I had a great deal of the bowling and we took 31 of the 51 wickets which fell.

Not quite all of my time doing National Service was spent playing cricket. I was mustered as a PT instructor and did my three months' training at West Drayton and then up at Cosford, near Wolverhampton. There, I developed cartilage trouble playing football and had to go into hospital for several weeks. Once that ordeal was over, I was sent to Chessington to rehabilitate, which suited me well because it was near enough to home to warrant a living out pass. In fact, for the majority of the time I was serving in the RAF, I was living at home. The difficulty was not getting up when reveille sounded, but getting up at home in time to make the journey back to camp.

In a way, it was a good thing not to live on the camp because there is no denying that sportsmen had privileged lives as national servicemen. I could not have blamed any of the other less fortunate conscripts who resented this, so it was perhaps just as well that I was not sharing a hut with them.

While I was recovering at Chessington and at home, I decided not to go ahead with my PTI course. Carrying on would have meant another 16–18 weeks of rigorous training, during which I would not get any time off for cricket. So I packed it in and I was wondering what step to take next to make sure my cricket boots did not grow mouldy through lack of use, when I remembered Air Vice-Marshall Sharp. I wrote to him at once, telling him what had happened to me, and he immediately arranged to have me posted back to West Drayton. The adjutant there, Flight Lieutenant Cox, sent me, very sensibly, I thought, to work in the sports section. Apart from him and the people in the section, I don't honestly think anyone knew I was there.

Once again, I played for the RAF at Lord's against the Army and the Navy. Freddie Trueman was in the team that summer along with Jim Pressdee and Roy Swetman. We also went on a tour of Holland and Germany, which gave me my first experience of playing on mats. It was a pleasant trip and I got to know a lot of young county players my own age through it.

I did not spend very much time at West Drayton that summer. Apart from the matches and the tour, I also played in several games for Middlesex, including the fixture against the Indian touring team, and in several more for the Second XI. I can't really believe that the nation benefited greatly from my presence in the armed services and, in spite of the amount of cricket I played, I think the feeling was mutual. Two years spent doing something you are not really interested in is quite a slice out of anyone's life. Yet I am hardly in a position to complain, when so many older players had their careers interrupted for much longer by the war, and so many others failed to return. I recall I did consider that sobering thought, telling myself quite firmly not to start feeling too sorry for myself. After all, when my National Service came to an end, I was still only just past my 20th birthday and the cricket season was looming once again.

As the new 1953 season opened, I was delighted to be selected for the first county match against Northants at Peterborough, and I went on to play in all but two of the Championship games that summer. That first match was memorable because we thought our chances had gone when, in a sensational twist, it ended in a tie. Northants needed just two runs to win with three wickets left, when Bill Edrich put himself on to bowl to show that he had conceded defeat. In his time, Bill was, of course, a bowler who was good enough to open the England attack, which he had done in South Africa before the war, but in 1953 he had virtually given up bowling.

To everyone's surprise, not least his own, Bill promptly bowled out RW Clarke but, with Des Barrick at 80 not out at the other end, we still did not expect to avoid defeat. However, when the scores were level, Les Compton stumped Starkie off Jack Young. Then Des Barrick played a nervous maiden to Bill and Jack clean bowled Fiddling for a duck and, to the amazement of all concerned, the home team had failed to clinch a 'certain' victory and the match was a rare tie.

It was early in 1953 that I decided to abandon my seamers and concentrate on bowling off-breaks. In the RAF and in my early matches for Middlesex, I had alternated between the two types of bowling. At that time, I was really more of a batsman but the fact I could bowl helped and, gradually, my bowling came on. I didn't really decide to try to make it as an all-rounder, I just always did both.

In those early days, I bowled seamers at a slowish-medium pace. I was reasonably good but then I tried bowling slow and I found I was instantly more effective. I changed pretty quickly to being an off-spinner and hardly ever bowled another seam ball at all. Accuracy is vital to a spin bowler and I think all the years of practising in the play area near the flat where we lived paid off for me. I often used to go out on my own and just bowl at the wicket.

To be frank, I think I thought that if I stuck to the pace stuff there was too much competition with Alan Moss, John Warr and Don Bennett all regularly in the side. I consulted wise old Jack Robertson before I made my final decision, though. I recall moaning, 'I don't see any future as a seamer, Jack… getting the ball when it's all battered and then trying to take wickets.' He agreed and backed up my decision to switch to off-breaks.

Bill Edrich also approved as I nervously took advantage of the great experience in the side and, in the Whitsun match against Sussex, the new policy began. It did not produce outstanding results at once. I had 2 wickets for 81 in that match. But it had paid off by the end of the season. I took 105 wickets for an average of 24.

We used to play Sussex on a Bank Holiday at Hove; we would finish the game on Saturday at half-past six and Denis would be gone by quarter-past seven. He was off to stay with his pal Lord Porchester who lived just down the road in Hampshire, One Monday morning he hadn't arrived back in time for play. We were in the field, and Rev David Sheppard and Jimmy Parks were getting some runs. At about a quarter-to-one, Denis arrived. Just three-quarters of an hour before lunch. He wandered on to the field without proper kit – he was wearing some tennis shoes because he had lost his boots somewhere.

Bill, the captain, was his big pal and the first thing Denis said was not a word of apology or excuse for his absence, but, 'I've got three winners for this afternoon off Porchy.' My pal John Murray used to hear all this because Bill was first slip in those days and John was the wicket keeper. Denis was always second slip.

They couldn't wait to get off the field at lunchtime to look at the paper to see the odds and gets their bets on. But back on the field the Rev and Jim were going well, so Bill put Denis on to bowl and he got both of them out and another wicket before lunch. What a man. That's how we played the game. They weren't interested in whether or not we won the Championship. They had seen war for six years so you could understand them not being too worried about the result of a cricket match.

While I was away in the RAF, the county captaincy had passed to Bill Edrich. I liked Bill, largely because he let me bowl a lot. Any captain who did that was bound to endear himself instantly to me. I always disliked having nothing to do in the field and not being in the game. I always thought that standing at mid-off with only the occasional drive to stop was pretty tedious. Bill gave me plenty of work and, as I was very young at the time, this was good for me. Bill was a good skipper who never got in a flap and never lost his temper. If he wanted to tell you off, he would do it tactfully.

I remember once I was batting with him and he told me to stop flashing at balls outside the off-stump. Eventually, impatient and eager to get at the bowling, I flashed again with the inevitable result. Later, Bill called me out of the dressing room and quietly ticked me off. There are some captains who bawl players out in front of the entire side with the idea, I suppose, of making an example of them. This very old-fashioned approach to discipline never did appeal to me and I don't think it is ever likely to bring the best out of anyone.

The Australians were over that year and Len Hutton's team regained the Ashes after the Aussies had held them for almost 19 years. For the first time I played against the Australians, but not in the Tests. The Middlesex match in mid-July was spoiled by rain and the tourists used it, on the second and third days, as batting practice. I caught and bowled Richie Benaud and also got de Courcy and, in our first innings, I managed to collect a dozen runs before Ray Lindwall bowled me. I was rather disappointed with my batting that year as I didn't even score a 50. But it was encouraging to take 100 wickets for the first time and to be awarded my county cap.

In the middle of June, I had one of those purple patches when everything goes just right. I took 30 wickets in a fortnight and we won three out of four matches. But I found, not for the first or the last time, that my best performance – 8 for 53 at Bristol – was in a game we lost.

While I was doing my National Service, John Murray made his first appearance for Middlesex. He was a little younger than me and joined the county just after me; over the years, we became very close. He was a fine wicket-keeper and an excellent batsman who hit the ball very hard. John has always been a very relaxed and cheerful person to have around and I'm happy to say that, as we ease into our seventies, we are still good friends who enjoy each other's company.

Back in the early 1950s, I discovered that John had a particularly fine cricketing brain and, from his unique vantage point, he was always able to judge my bowling better than anyone else. When things were not going well,

John was always the first person I would turn to for advice and he never let me down.

I had cartilage trouble but I hid it for a long time because I wanted to keep my place. If you drop out of the side, you let someone else in. My football injury meant that my knee used to get locked, so I used to wear rubber boots instead of spikes, and quite often I would wear rubber on one foot and spikes on the other to save pressure on my turning knee. I got away with it. And I was helped by Bill Tucker, the best physio in the business, who also happened to be an orthopaedic surgeon. He was a former rugby international and a great bloke.

The 1954 season brought two personal landmarks – I took 100 wickets for Middlesex in county Championship matches alone and I was twelfth man for England in the second Test against Pakistan. This was not only the second Test of the season, but also the second official Test ever played against Pakistan . It would normally have been played at Lord's but tradition demanded that the first official Test against any new cricketing country had to be played at headquarters, so the second match in the series was at Trent Bridge.

I was very proud to be selected for the whole Test and not simply as one of 12 or 13 players who became twelfth man because he'd been left out. But, to be truthful, it was not a very arduous task. I didn't even get on the field to take out the drinks. The year of 1954 was one of those cold summers when it was rarely hot enough to stop the game for refreshment.

The England team was captained by the Rev David Sheppard, who was still in with a chance of leading the MCC in Australia the following winter. Len Hutton had been injured in the first game and David and Reg Simpson opened with an assault on the Pakistan attack, which was carried on by Denis Compton and Tom Graveney. Denis had an inspired time. He reached 200 in 245 minutes and batted for 290 minutes in all, to reach his highest Test total of 278. I stood in rapt admiration as Denis hammered a six and 33 fours before being bowled by 16-year-old Khalid Hassan.

It was a truly memorable innings in many ways. I particularly recall that the Test was played during Wimbledon fortnight and we were watching the men's final as Denis went in to bat. If the match ended while he was in, Denis wanted the result to be signalled to him. Drobny duly won and someone went on to the balcony and gave Denis the thumbs up sign. Soon after this, he really began to see the ball clearly and the runs piled up even more rapidly. At the end of the day, we were all listening to Jim Swanton's summing up on the day's play. He referred to the turning point of the innings when a message was signalled to Compton to open up. Swanton was always a shade pompous in his pronouncements and this caused some amusement. He couldn't have been expected to know about Denis's bet, but it just shows how wrong you can be when you try to interpret the mysterious signs that players sometimes make to one another.

David Sheppard became a good friend and I came to admire the way he combined his faith with his sport. He once invited me to speak to the boys of his youth club attached to the church in Islington where he then preached. I talked as best as I could about my attitude to religion, which was mostly recalled from my Sunday school days, and then answered questions. The questions were mercifully mostly connected with cricket but the occasion was evidently regarded as a success because, afterwards, I was deluged with invitations from various chapels and churches scattered all around north London. I accepted many of them and usually found them interesting, but I did draw the line when the organisers of a huge religious rally in a stadium at Willesden requested my presence on the platform. It was one thing to talk to David's boys in a church hall, and quite another to face an expected 14,000 congregation in a vast arena. I did not see myself as a Billy Graham figure and that put an end to my career as a preacher.

On the county front, my admiration for Denis Compton grew and grew that year. He celebrated his 35th birthday on 23 May by scoring a brilliant unbeaten 143 against Sussex at Lord's. He hit 17 fours and his last 40 runs came in just 20 minutes.

Middlesex had an unhappy habit of starting the season like a runaway train and then having their results derailed somewhere about mid-summer. In 1954, everything was going wonderfully as we won our first six matches but then allowed our chances of winning the Championship to slip away with a sequence of indifferent results. Poor Denis missed quite a lot of the season with a combination of Test calls, knee trouble and lumbago. I was delighted that my friend John Murray was becoming established as our regular wicket-keeper as Denis's brother, Leslie, headed for retirement.

Leslie had been the regular keeper since 1947, when he had taken over from the highly-rated Fred Price. He is better remembered as a footballer for Arsenal and England but, behind the stumps, he had one of the safest pairs of hands in the game. He was a solid, reliable keeper rather than any sort of a showman and, while he was never the greatest of stumpers, he often gave me reason to be glad that he was there to snap up the chances. When he retired, he sent a telegram to his successor John Murray which read, 'I took over from a great wicket-keeper. You are taking over from a wicket-keeper who liked keeping wicket. Good luck.'

The county did suffer a miserable August which was highlighted by a resounding 96-run victory over Yorkshire at Headingley which caused me great satisfaction. Norman Yardley put us in to bat and he seemed to have got the decision spot on as we struggled to reach 197 with John Dewes top-scoring with 45. But when Yorkshire batted, it was a similar story and, apart from a dogged 52 from Brian Close, the home side hit trouble and were all out for 113. Rain affected the pitch quite badly and the Middlesex second innings finished on just 131 thanks to Bob Appleyard picking up four cheap wickets.

So Yorkshire needed to score 216 to win and Jack Young and yours truly combined well to give them no chance. Jack finished with 4 wickets for 53 runs while I managed 6 for 50. It was an unexpected victory and it was all the more pleasing because it was against Yorkshire. The crowd, which normally cheers the home side loudly every inch of the way, was very quiet by the end. Silence really was golden.

Middlesex drifted to a pretty meaningless seventh place in the County Championship but I did have one final high note to my season in the match against the touring Pakistan side. We lost by 140 runs in the end but I had two good knocks, of 54 not out and 61. I really felt that I had arrived as a cricketer. Middlesex finished fifth in the County Championship. I took 111 wickets for an average of 20.45 that year and life felt great. I was 21 years old and making a living playing the game I loved. Who could ask for anything more?

Well, me, for one; in February 1955, I married Jean Marriott, moved out to the leafy suburbs of Enfield and we went on to have two lovely children, Dawn and Mark.

On the cricket field, there were other great developments. An England call was something I never quite dared let myself expect. I just kept plugging away but, at the end of May, I knew I had done myself some good when I came off for the MCC against the touring South Africans. It was an exciting match at Lord's and, in the second innings, I managed to get 8 wickets for 43 runs, including a spell of the last 5 wickets for just 3 runs in 7 overs. Some days, everything goes right and this was one of them.

I was delighted to be chosen to play for England against South Africa. I heard the good news from my mum. The press broke it to her and she ran up the road to a telephone box and rang me even before I had been notified officially. I thought it was a wonderful surprise.

My England début was at Lord's on 23 June. We won the match by 71 runs and Denis Compton scored his 5,000th Test run. I scored 4 and 16 with the bat and took one wicket for 50, but I bowled reasonably tidily and fielded enthusiastically and, evidently, I did enough to keep my place for the next Test at Old Trafford.

Playing with Denis Compton was always full of surprises. In my second Test match for England, I was down to go in number seven, but when I saw Denis striding confidently to the wicket ahead of me at his favourite number four, I noticed to my horror that he was carrying my favourite old NAAFI bat. Denis was never one for elaborate preparations. He would just pick up a bat and go out and look brilliant. He certainly was that day as he fashioned 158 stylish runs before he was caught. As luck would have it, I was next in, so I collected my bat from Denis on my way to the wicket. Sadly, I did not need it for long, being out lbw to Heine, without, as they say, troubling the scorer. On the long walk back to the pavilion, I was almost off the pitch when some sharp Mancunian shouted, 'Compton's bat didn't do you much good, did it?' I was going to explain that it was my bat, but common sense prevented me starting a long conversation.

I did score 19 in the second innings but we lost a close match by 3 wickets. Godfrey Evans fractured a finger, yet still shared with Trevor Bailey a brave last wicket stand of 48 that might have saved the match.

Sadly, after that I was dropped. The captain, Peter May, was criticised for not giving me a fair chance with England, but I have always felt I was fairly treated. Peter May was only three years older than me and he was very new to the captaincy. He had inherited the job unexpectedly after Len Hutton's sudden retirement and we were facing a very fine South African side. In his first rubber as skipper, he was understandably anxious to win. He must have believed his Surrey colleague Jim Laker was the best off-spinner in the country and he was brought in to the fifth Test and took 7 for 84. I took one wicket for 101 in my two first Tests. I am a firm believer in figures and, in this case, there was no way I could make them add up in my favour.

I refused to be down-hearted and told myself that my chance would come again. Of course, I didn't realise then that it was going to take seven years to arrive, but I contented myself with getting my head down and playing well for Middlesex. At the end of August, in fact, I played for my county against the touring South Africans in a match I remember most vividly thanks to the highly individual fielding of Denis Compton. I was always slightly uneasy about Denis on the field when I was bowling and he was fielding at mid-off or mid-on. Like Ted Dexter, Denis wanted things to happen the whole time; he couldn't stand the game going to sleep. If it did, he would be full of gratuitous advice to you to – 'Throw one up' – which I could generally do without. He was also practically impossible to place on the field unless you put him very close to the wicket so that he couldn't very well wander about.

I was bowling to the free-scoring Winslow when Denis got tremendous applause for what was certainly a very spectacular catch. Winslow slammed the ball hard and high towards the boundary over mid-off. Denis leapt several feet up to his left and took the catch one-handed. It was a brilliant catch, I'll give him that, but if he had stayed in the position I had asked him to take up, he wouldn't have had to move at all!

I finally gave up playing football. After my cartilage operation, I was never quite as effective at soccer and, although I enjoyed playing, it seemed wise to concentrate on just one game. It might seem hard to believe but, in those days, cricketers were better paid than footballers, though neither sport produced too many millionaires. And there was always the ever-present example of Denis Compton and his painful knee as a constant warning of what could happen to footballer-cricketers.

Happily, Tests apart, I had a very good season with the ball and beat the Middlesex record of 154 wickets set by Albert Trott 55 years earlier. At the end of the season, a total of 191 Titmus wickets at an average of 16.31 left me very proud and very tired. I also managed to do the 'double' of 1,000 runs and 100 wickets. Remarkably, I was the first Middlesex player to achieve this since RWV Robins and NE Haig back in 1929.

It was an extraordinary season. Against Somerset at Bath, the scene of my début some six years earlier, I took 15 wickets for 95 runs in the match and still finished on the losing side; I also scored 61 against Hampshire when several of our batsmen failed to deliver. Denis Compton's knee was restricting his appearances even more and he missed well over half the Middlesex season. But Denis still managed the occasional flash of brilliance.

We played Sussex on Whit Monday at Hove and he thrashed 150 runs out of 195 in our first innings before he was caught on the boundary by Suttle off Marlar. It was sublime cricket and the crowd of 20,000 stood to cheer him all the way back to the pavilion.

The other memorable triumph for me was a repeat victory over Yorkshire at Headingley in August. The Leeds wicket was damaged by rain and Yorkshire struggled to a meagre 151 after we put them in. We just exceeded that score despite some fine fast bowling from Freddie Trueman, who took 4 for 52, and Mike Cowan, who finished with 6 for 52. But Jack Young and I managed to spin Yorkshire out for 175, leaving us to score 168 to win. There were one or two dodgy moments, but we did it and achieved a win by five wickets.

4

A TESTING TOUR

At the end of the 1955 season, I was highly delighted to be invited to go on an MCC 'A' tour of Pakistan. The Test matches were to be unofficial but, to me, it was an instant compensation for having given up football.

The *SS Circassia* sailed from Liverpool on Saturday, 3 December 1955. On board were 15 mainly young cricketers led by captain Donald Carr of Derbyshire. We were full of high hopes of success in the sunshine far away from the English winter. Sadly, somehow, it did not turn out quite like that. It was a tour that began with high hopes of friendship between nations and finished with a team guarded by armed soldiers at the centre of an international incident.

To be fair, the omens were far from good from the start. On the way out, we docked at Aden. It had not rained locally for more than a year but, as if to celebrate our arrival, it absolutely pelted down, so the planned nets sessions were cancelled. The following month, a similar thing happened at Hyderabad. It had not rained there for two years, but the second and third days of our match were completely washed out by a downpour.

We started the tour in Karachi on Boxing Day with a match against the local cricket association, followed by a match against the Governor General's XI. They were both played on a peculiar-looking mat, on a green patch some 30 yards square, set on a little mound in the middle of a stretch of desert. This was the best mat we had played on and we did well in the opening games.

We won the second match against what was a strong side. In fact, it was effectively the Pakistan Test XI and, in retrospect, many of us realised this victory was a tactical error. It instantly antagonised our hosts and it meant that all the umpiring was much more hostile than the expected level of moderate bias in favour of the home sides.

Pakistan was only seven years old as an independent state and its people were very conscious of their national pride. Cricket was then and, to an extent, remains an important symbol of this pride. It mattered very much to the people of Pakistan that they did well in this series of unofficial Test matches. In fact, to the home side, there was nothing remotely unofficial about them.

Things have improved greatly since but, in the winter of 1955/6, the decisions from the men in the middle had to be seen to be believed. Our front-footed players suffered particularly. Jim Parks was given out lbw 7 times in 15 innings and all the decisions were made against him when his foot was down the wicket with the ball moving in off the seam. He was also the victim of an outrageous stumping when he stepped out of his crease to a very wide ball. He let it go, put his bat back and then watched the keeper take off the bails... and the umpire raise his finger.

Even off the field, life was interesting. We had a trip one day right up towards the Khyber Pass and on this very narrow dirt road we me met a stream of guys on horseback all armed to the teeth with guns slung over their shoulders. They looked very impressive and, although we had been told not to take any photographs, that's exactly what we stopped and did. We got out of the bus and took our cameras out. As soon as we did that, all these guys on horseback started pointing their rifles at us, so we decided that photography was not such a good idea. We jumped back in the bus and roared off.

In my opinion, dodgy decisions marred the tour. In a minor game at Hyderabad, I was dismissed 'run out' in a similar situation to Jim's at Karachi. The decisions always seemed to go against us but the facts were rarely mentioned in the press back home. Newspapers were a great deal less sensationalist in those days. In the Peshawar 'Test' I was given out 'caught at the wicket' when I had not even played at the ball. Crawford White, the *News Chronicle* cricket correspondent, came up to me afterwards and said, 'You weren't within a mile of that, Fred.' I agreed, but Crawford did not report it. The press were being uncharacteristically diplomatic at the time.

The Pakistani batsmen never seemed to suffer in the same way. Hanif Mohammad, their star opener and a cricketer of undeniable class, was naturally difficult to shift. At times on this tour, we felt that if we didn't send his middle stump flying or take an indisputable catch off him, it was virtually impossible to get him out. We were convinced we had him leg before wicket on a couple of occasions in every innings because he regularly padded the ball away while standing plumb in front of his stumps.

The other class player they had was Fazal Mahmood, who was largely responsible for Pakistan's victory over England at The Oval in 1954. He bowled very fast leg cutters on the mat in a style reminiscent of Alec Bedser, and then he would occasionally surprise us with an off-cutter. He and Hanif were the only outstanding players we faced.

The biased umpiring rather set the scene for a difficult atmosphere on this tour. The players were mainly in their early twenties and full of high spirits. But in Pakistan at that time there was no social life, apart from a series of very fussy formal receptions. The food was strange to us and we were inclined to adopt a siege mentality by buying in eggs and potatoes and preparing ourselves many meals of egg and chips. We couldn't drink the water without being pretty sure of contracting a stomach bug and the beer was prohibitively expensive at nine shillings a bottle.

But all of this was no real excuse for the prank that soured the tour still further – the soaking of umpire Idris Begh. He was an immaculately-dressed chap who, like most of his colleagues, seemed to me to favour the home side more than he should have done. He could be a good umpire but I thought he was more than a little biased.

We hadn't got on very well with Idris. To be brutally frank, we thought he had stuffed us here and there. Up in Peshawar, near the border, we stayed in this large rambling hotel that was more like a block of flats. Idris came to have a drink with Donald Carr and some retribution was organised. Above the door of the room they were in there was a ventilation hole to let the air in to circulate. Some of the players put a chair under the ventilation hole and invited Idris to sit down. The bathroom was on the other side of the door. A small bowl of water was put up there and, while there were several of the boys involved, I think it was Roy Swetman who actually gave the bowl the final tip and poor old Idris was duly soaked.

He was a very smart, almost fancy, dresser but, at a stroke, his dignity was gone and he was absolutely furious. Donald Carr put his arm round him and tried to talk him round, saying, 'Don't storm off all wet, Idris. We've done this to other umpires and they've got really upset but you've treated it like a champion.'

But he wasn't having it and he marched angrily out. Inevitably, it made the press and the next thing we knew our hotel had a crowd of 1,000 Pakistanis wanting to get us. We had to play the next match with a ring of armed soldiers and police round the ground, and there were demonstrations as the Test proceeded. Students rallied with banners and shouted, 'Go home MCC.' Considering we were supposed to be cricketing missionaries on a goodwill trip aimed at fostering friendly relations, this was not exactly good news.

It wasn't really a very happy time. Lord Alexander of Tunis was president of the MCC and he telephoned the manager, Geoffrey Howard, and asked if the boys ought to come home. Geoffrey Howard was a lovely old chap and he looked pained as he got us all together and told us gravely, 'Lord Alexander thinks you ought to come home. What do you think?'

The response was inevitable. 'Three cheers for Lord Alexander.' It was not a very happy tour.

Geoffrey said, 'Don't be silly, boys, I've straightened it all out now.' Cables of apology flashed backwards and forwards between Pakistan and England and it was decided, way above our heads, that the tour should continue.

After the Peshawar 'ducking', we were given protection. We went out sightseeing in the town when we noticed we were being followed by a serious-looking little man. We decided to challenge him. 'I am your bodyguard,' he said, 'in case there is trouble.' He patted his side and revealed a .45 Colt pistol strapped to his hip.

But then there was a sledging incident in the last match involving Pakistan batsman Imtiaz Ahmed. It was all something about nothing but it was blown into a huge diplomatic incident. First Imtiaz, who was also their wicket-keeper, claimed a 'catch' against Jim Parks. I was batting at the other end and saw the ball bounce a yard or two in front of Imtiaz who then gathered it and their players appealed loudly... and successfully. Jim looked disgusted and walked.

I went over to Idris Begh, who was standing at square leg, and asked him if he had witnessed what Parks and I had seen clearly. He said it was not his decision, so I walked quickly back to his colleague, who had by then realised his error. 'Oh, Mr Titmus,' he said, 'all umpires make mistakes.' He had time to rectify this one, though, by calling Jim back, but he didn't do so.

After that, the tension between the teams grew. When Pakistan were batting, I was bowling to Imtiaz and made two appeals for leg before wicket which were both disallowed. Someone fielding close to the wicket expressed his disappointment with the umpire's decision in strong language. Now, everyone who plays first-class cricket knows that a certain amount of swearing goes on. We don't all swear, but we do all recognise that it happens. On this occasion, Imtiaz complained about it through our liaison officer. It was all smoothed over but we were left feeling rather niggled because the liaison officer told us that the Pakistani players also swore, only they did it in Urdu so none of us ever knew.

In cricketing terms, there were still plenty of enjoyable

moments. On our side Tony Lock had a great tour, taking 81 wickets at an average of 10.72. He was very popular off the field – more perhaps, considering his figures – than on it! The Pakistani people treated Tony like a little god. When we stopped at railways stations on our way from fixture to fixture, the crowd would be lined up waiting for us. As we drew in, they would chant, 'We want Tony Lock, we want Tony Lock.' Tony responded like a natural actor. He put a cigarette in a long holder and leant out of the window with all the dignity of a true English lord to receive the homage of his people. It was a great sight.

My Middlesex colleague Alan Moss also did well, taking 41 wickets for 17.48, and I came third in quantity with 28 for 23.25. If anything, I did better with the bat. I found the matting suited my style of play and I scored 457 runs for an average of 30.46. I loved to employ cut strokes and these seemed to come off well in Pakistan. I tried to avoid the lbw dangers by not doing too much front foot stuff and I did develop a new stroke while on tour which became known among my friends as 'Fred's Pakistani'. It was a sort of slash drive and I got away with it so long as the ball did not come through too fast. I would be half forward and play a cross-bat swipe somewhere past cover. Exactly where past cover was nobody's business, but it was my stroke.

The papers back home were full of pompous editorials and all the players were bound by contract which decreed that they could not even speak about the tour for a further

12 months. The real problem was that Idris and his pals only ever saw things one way and that was against the tourists. There was virtually no chance of getting anyone out lbw. In fact, unless you splattered the stumps in all directions, our opponents stayed in. As we headed for home, the flak flew in the direction of our manager Geoffrey Howard, the Lancashire secretary, and our captain Donald Carr, who had to carry the can for our misdemeanours. It was unfortunate because they were both fine men who did difficult jobs very well in trying circumstances.

There is a little known sequel to the Idris Begh incident, in that we struck a tie for Idris which showed a finger being raised to signify a batsman being given out. Underneath, there were the initials 'IB'. I have never seen anyone wear it and it may even be officially banned. I don't know about that, but I still have mine at home as a memento. Or perhaps, I should say, as a reminder of how not to behave.

The tour ended as strangely as it had begun. After four months away from home, we were all anxious to get back as soon as possible. Mercifully, we were flying back but the plane took off from Karachi some nine irritating hours behind schedule. At Baghdad, there was a further delay because the plane had developed engine trouble. We touched down somewhere else and were then hurriedly diverted because the residents were rioting. Next, we landed in Beirut and were disembarked into a large glass control tower right on the airfield. Billy Sutcliffe observed wearily, 'All we want now is a bloody earthquake.' Within ten seconds, there was a great tremor. Glass fell out of the tower and the building instantly emptied of people. We were still pretty fit then, and the MCC side were the first out. Certainly, we all moved faster than we had done at any time in Pakistan. The earthquake did do some serious damage in other areas but, fortunately for us, we were soon back on our plane and away. Somehow, a natural disaster seemed to be a fitting end to a largely disastrous tour.

In the 1956 season, there was only one off-spinner making headlines… and it wasn't me. First, Jim Laker took all ten wickets in an innings for county champions Surrey against the Australians at The Oval in mid-May, and then he did it again for England in the Fourth Test at Old Trafford at the end of July, where he finished the match with 19 wickets for 90 – a record that is unlikely ever to be beaten.

On that kind of form, I was never going to get a look in as far as England were concerned but, ten days after Laker's first triumph, I did play against the Aussies for the MCC at Lord's. The Saturday of the match was one of the few warm sunny days we had in that dismal summer, and we toiled for six hours in the heat while Neil Harvey batted brilliantly towards a double century. The second wicket did not fall until half-past-five, when Alan Moss got Rutherford leg before, but on the Monday I had some success and finished with 5 for 130, which included the wickets of Richie Benaud, Keith Miller and Ray Lindwall.

I met the Australians again in July when they came to headquarters to play Middlesex. We started late with the pitch still drying out from the sort of soaking it received many times that dismal summer, and I had a much better Saturday than before when Neil Harvey was thumping the ball about with such abandon. I had him caught by Hurst when he had scored only 11 that day, and I got five wickets for exactly half of what they had cost me in the earlier fixture. But by then, Jim Laker was busily amassing his record total of 46 Test wickets in a series and, quite rightly, no one was thinking about including me in the England side.

At Middlesex, John Murray had great success in his first full season. With Leslie Compton now out of the picture, John really took his chance and he claimed 77 victims (63 caught and 14 stumped) in all matches, which was more than any other wicket-keeper in the country. He also developed a talent for opening and hit a spirited 48 against Gloucestershire at Lord's. A young batsman called Peter Parfitt also came through, along with Ron Hooker, as the year saw the team begin some major line-up changes. Peter came into the side on the recommendation of Bill Edrich.

The Edrich family learned their cricket in Norfolk and Bill was in the county for a club match one Sunday when he saw Peter's precocious talent at first hand. He had heard a little about the young left-hander's brilliance as a schoolboy cricketer and he was so impressed by what he saw that Peter was invited to join the staff at Lord's. Bob

Gale also came into the side that year, and so did another player who was to become a county stalwart – Eric Russell. As far as my own form went, without ever quite reaching the heights of the previous year, I managed to do the 'double' again and fell four short of another century when we went up to Cambridge. This saw the start of lifelong friendships with these new, young players.

Denis Compton's knee injury worsened and he had to have his right knee-cap removed. But despite his limp, Denis scored 110 at Glastonbury and 101 against Kent at Lord's and won back his England place against the Australians at The Oval where the old master scored 94 and 35 not out. Old cricketers have an uplifting habit of defying the obituarists who are anxious to write them off. Bill Edrich reached his fortieth birthday in 1956, but he topped the averages and managed a stirring double century against Derbyshire at Chesterfield.

The 1957 season was marked by the retirement from full-time cricket of the famous Middlesex 'twins', Denis Compton and Bill Edrich. Time defeats everyone in the end, but it was still a desperately sad time when two such fine cricketers neared the end. Denis had been through three operations on his knee and his mobility was greatly reduced. It was sad to see him struggling, though, typically, he still scored three stylish centuries in the season. He hit 143 against Worcestershire at Lord's, 109 against Essex at Leyton and 104 at Old Trafford against Lancashire, and topped the county averages with 1,404 championship runs.

Jack Robertson was also coming to the end of an illustrious career, although he did not finally bow out until 1959, and he fired another blow for the 40-year-olds by scoring a wonderful double-hundred against Essex at Lord's in July. He registered an unbeaten 201 which included 17 fours.

Alan Moss and I had a good day with the ball to finish Essex off. Personally, I was delighted to do the double for the third successive season, but I was even more pleased when John Murray marked his arrival as a real force to be reckoned with behind the stumps. As a model of consistency, John became only the second wicket-keeper in history to score more than 1,000 runs and dismiss over 100 batsmen in a season.

I had the chance to witness John's improvement with the bat at close hand when we put on 82 at Dover in August. That was an extraordinary match as Alan Moss and I managed to bowl Kent out for just 108, only to find ourselves struggling again at 86 for 6 before I was able to come to the rescue with a knock of 70, which featured 2 sixes and 9 fours. I certainly enjoyed that. Then, with personal figures of 7 for 24, Alan Moss bowled Kent out for 43 almost single-handedly, to leave Middlesex victors by 231 runs. It's not just football that is a funny old game. We finished seventh in the table and the retirement of Bill Edrich left us without a skipper.

John Murray was the man I spoke to the most about all aspects of the game. I was so lucky to be bowling to one of the best wicket-keepers in England. Peter Parfitt was certainly the best first slip in England; he could catch sparrows if they flew near enough. And Ron Hooker was the best short-leg. And I had all three of them helping me to get wickets. I was very fortunate.

I got a lot of advice from John Murray, and only some of it is printable. We were always very straight and direct with each other as true friends can be. 'You're not bowling very well today, Titmus,' he would say if I strayed very far from the line. 'You're not keeping very well today, Murray,' I would say if there was the remotest hint of a fumble. We kept each other on our toes.

If a quick one did happen to get past Peter Parfitt, I could never resist pointing it out. 'We haven't woken you up, have we, Parfitt?' I would call and be sure of a swift reply. But the three of them were brilliant.

Quick bowler John Warr took over as captain of a Middlesex side still very much in a transitional stage at the onset of the 1958 season. John had been in the team since 1949 and had toured Australia with Brown's team in 1950–51. He was a very experienced player and he had the advantage that a very young captain can never have, of knowing all the people in the game. If you have been playing for nine seasons, as John had when he took over as skipper, you have built up a fair knowledge of practically everyone else in the county sides. You know the weaknesses of particular players and the oddities of particular grounds. This must help considerably in the sheer technique of captaincy. Not even the greatest can rely on inspiration the whole time and, in my view, John was technically the best captain in the country at that time. He was not the world's finest fielder, but this did not seriously hamper his authority because he was very enthusiastic and had a keen understanding of just how much he could expect from each player. If you fell below the standard he knew you were capable of reaching, then you heard about it. He often joked about my habit of talking on the field and claimed he never quite got used to my taking a slip catch in mid-conversation.

We drew no fewer than 16 of our 28 games and finished tenth in the Championship. A dull season was enlivened by an exciting finish against Leicestershire when our opponents needed just six runs to win when stumps were drawn. The finish became shrouded in controversy when the pavilion clock chose just the wrong moment to stop!

The sun shone brightly throughout a glorious summer for cricket, but the 1959 season saw Middlesex still frequently finding runs hard to come by. However, we did win the £500 prize for the fastest 200 in a first innings in the season with a bright start at Trent Bridge in August. Middlesex eventually declared at 397 for 9 and won by 74 runs after I was able to take 7 for 64 in Nottinghamshire's second innings. I did the double again with 1,242 runs and 102 wickets in Championship games after bowling more than 1,000 overs in the season.

The season opened with a very exciting game. Middlesex were all out for 203 against Kent at Lord's, only for Colin Cowdrey to cut loose in the second innings with 3 sixes and 8 fours. It was very close when last man Page came to the wicket as Kent still needed 20 runs with a quarter-of-an-hour remaining. Eight minutes later, Page and Brown had whittled that down to three runs and then I was able to make Brown drag a ball on to his stumps and we won by two runs.

Jack Robertson was the last member of the great pre-war side to retire. He carried on until he took his second benefit which had an unexpected effect on me because, in one of the draws, I won a car. At the time I couldn't drive and, during home matches, I was in danger of getting a reputation for being slightly unsociable as I used to cycle or catch the bus home to Enfield rather then staying for a drink with the boys. The car was a great help in getting me around and I found I was able to stay around and often enjoy the genial company in the Star at St John's Wood after the day's play at Lord's. The landlord of the pub, Bill Jones, was a great Middlesex supporter and I began to enjoy the social side of cricket much more than in my earlier years. Some readers might be surprised that there was a time when Fred Titmus did not particularly enjoy a drink. They should content themselves with the knowledge that he has more than made up for lost time since!

I was beginning to build up a good deal of experience, and something of a reputation for myself as a solid performer and, in the late 1950s, I was delighted to take up the opportunity of escaping the chill of the English winter by travelling to the sunshine of South Africa to do some cricket coaching. The first invitation came from the Christian Brothers College at Kimberley, and it was quite an experience.

I arrived to meet the remarkable Brother Reidy who had been in charge of cricket in the area for the preceding 50 years. He was well over 80 and, not surprisingly, we did not always see eye to eye over coaching methods. Fortunately for me, the college came top of the local league for the first time in 30 years in my first season, so that rather strengthened my position. I helped to strengthen their side by playing for them, which was not as unfair as it sounds because this was a men's league and the college team was, apart from me, all boys.

Brother Reidy was a great character locally. He had become a very well-known figure riding around on his ancient upright bicycle on which he displayed a hearty disrespect for all traffic laws. He was once challenged by a youthful policeman after he rode through a red traffic light. In his thick Irish brogue, he brushed aside the officer's objections, saying, 'I was here before the lights, wasn't I?' Once he was so ill that the last rites were gravely administered but, within a week, he was up and about riding around on his bike.

South Africa is a beautiful country and I came to love the weather, the wide open spaces and the wonderfully resourceful people. I particularly recall being asked to visit the Elizabeth Conradie School for handicapped Children in Kimberley. I talked to them about cricket as requested, but it was hard to take their smiles in the face of the sort of crippling conditions which would always prevent many of them from ever enjoying my game. The children expressed their appreciation by presenting me with a pewter plaque of a child's head which they had made themselves. It remains one of my proudest possessions to this day.

Jimmy Gray of Hampshire recommended me for my next coaching job in South Africa. It was in a school run by the Western Province Cricket Union in Cape Town, and I also put some time in instructing the players at Cape Town university, who included a very talented young man called Peter Van de Merwe, who later went on to captain the South African national side. We struck up a friendship that has stood the test of time. I'll always be grateful to Jimmy for his help. He taught me more about coaching than anyone else, and more about golf into the bargain.

I played a lot of cricket for the Northerns team in the Peninsular Cup. They were predominantly an Afrikaaner side and, although there was traditionally some friction between the English and the Afrikaaners, I was always made very welcome and made many friends.

The pattern of my life took on a certain rhythm during the later 1950s and early 1960s. My winters were spent in the stimulating warmth of South Africa, while my summers were devoted to Middlesex. I did the 'double' every year but one, and played in every Championship match for Middlesex unless I was called upon by the MCC, although that did not happen very often as I only missed one county match in five years.

I found myself trapped in a cricketing 'no man's land' during this period. I had no fear of losing my place in the county side, but I did not seem to be getting any nearer the England team than when I came out of the RAF. In fact, I was further away because I had actually played for England twice in 1955. My life was becoming that of an average county player, travelling round the country playing on this ground and that and having a fair amount of success with both bat and ball, before packing my bags every autumn to head off and spend a winter in the sun. I realised that the danger was that I would become content and satisfied with this life. Many people spend large stretches of their lives in far less satisfying fashion, so I knew that, in the scheme of things, I had nothing to complain about.

But a cricketer's playing life is comparatively short, or so I believed at the time! You cannot wait and bide your time, like, perhaps, a politician or a businessman, in the hope that your major success will come in middle age. In cricketing terms, I was approaching 30 and that is middle age for a sportsman. Every cricketer knows that if he has not made the grade internationally by the time he is 30, then the odds are against him ever doing so. If he has not been chosen to tour Australia by then, he can probably write off the whole idea of international honours. I was starting seriously to consider that my England chances had come and gone with my two frustratingly unsatisfying appearances against South Africa.

In 1958, I had a poor season and, in any case, Jim Laker was still around, so I was not surprised not to be invited to join the party for Peter May's big tour Down Under. That was a season when I did not bowl as much as I normally did. I am very much a facts and figures man, and I do believe that statistics in cricket do tell quite a story. I was never greatly impressed by allegedly fine players whose career records show that, although they have played for England, they have never scored a century or taken five Test wickets in an innings. I never placed much store in gallant little innings of 25, or spells of bowling during which, if the player had not had a bit of bad luck, or if he'd not been let down by his field, he would have got wickets. The great players have always scored their runs and taken their wickets, whatever the circumstances. They may have had their luck – all players need their share of that – but they have also achieved results in terms of facts and figures. And you don't win Test matches by scoring 25 or taking 1 for 105.

Equally, you don't take wickets unless you bowl a sufficient number of overs. I used to estimate that, over a season, I needed to bowl ten overs to take a wicket. Without wishing to blow my trumpet too loudly, by the end of my career I think I managed a slightly better record, but ten overs a wicket was always a handy rule of thumb.

At the start of the Sixties, Middlesex at last made a serious challenge for the County Championship title. We started well by beating Hampshire by just one run with a cool John Murray hitting the winning stroke. Alan Moss had a great season, taking 114 wickets at a remarkable 12.5 runs apiece. The highlights of the season were two victories over close rivals Surrey, whom Middlesex had not beaten since 1948. At The Oval, we won the toss and made 284 for 7 declared before bowling out Surrey for 71 and 192. I took 5 for 24 in the first innings and we ran out winners by an innings and 21 runs.

Middlesex followed this famous victory up with an eight-wicket win at Lord's. This match marked the last appearance of the great Alec Bedser. Alec and I played together in his last Test match and struck up a great affinity which has lasted ever since. I still speak fairly regularly with Alec and his identical twin Eric, who was also a fine player. We discuss how times have changed and, in lighter moments, whether or not we would have fancied a nice winter trip to Zimbabwe! The Bedsers are two of the nicest people you could ever wish to meet. I the early years, I used to find it very hard to tell them apart, so I used to address each of them as 'Elic', for obvious reasons.

But having threatened to mount a challenge for the title, Middlesex were reduced to third place, thanks largely to a miserable draw against Worcestershire in the final match of the season.

By the end of the1960 season, I'd done the double five times in six seasons but, despite taking 6 for 86 for Middlesex against the touring New Zealanders, Yorkshire off-spinner Ray Illingworth jumped ahead of me in the off-spinner pecking order for England.

John Warr brought his spell as Middlesex captain to an end when he retired from first class cricket in 1961 and Ian Bedford was tempted back to Lord's to take charge of the side. The season began disastrously with defeats to Northants and Essex in the opening games. I took 5 wickets for 62 against Essex but they powered on to score 326 on an easy pitch and we were never really in the game. But after these early setbacks, we had a good run, winning 12 out of the next 15 matches and we soared from the bottom of the table to the top. Unfortunately, we then lost four games from the next seven and even a rousing finish, with victories over Yorkshire and Gloucestershire in the last two matches, could not win us the Championship. Middlesex finished third in the table again. In terms of figures, this was my best season to date, but it wasn't enough to help me win back my England place. That year, I was second in both the batting and bowling averages for Middlesex, scoring 1,501 runs at 36 and taking 123 wickets at 21.58.

I was disappointed not to be selected against Richie Benaud's Australian side, as I felt I was doing as well as most of the other spinners and the runs were certainly coming. But I was not chosen, as David Allen and Tony Lock did most of the slow bowling for England that summer. My friend John Murray did get his first cap, however, and I was delighted for John. Neither was I selected for that winter's tour of India, Pakistan and Ceylon, which saw my other close Middlesex pal Peter Parfitt begin his England career. Some 40 years later, Ted Dexter was president of the MCC when he asked me why on earth I had not gone on that tour. I was forced to reply, 'Because you didn't bloody well pick me!' To be honest, at the time I felt a little left out and I knuckled down to try to work really hard on my game. I realised that in 12 months time, in the summer of 1962, another party would be picked to tour Australia and, if I didn't get myself selected, I might have missed the boat in more ways than one with my plans for a glittering England career.

I never went to university myself, but I like to think I taught the students of Cambridge a thing or two when I had a great day at Fenners and took 9 for 52. Sir Len Hutton's son Richard was an early victim and one Michael Brearley was a later one. It was a very enjoyable day. Only my own pal Bob Gale spoiled my chance of getting all ten when he caught and bowled Pritchard for the last wicket. Some days, everything just clicks. But, in fact, that season Middlesex suffered a bowling crisis. Alan Moss's fine form dipped a little and Ron Hooker and Don Bennett were never able to offer quite enough support. It was with the bat where Peter Parfitt came into his own. He hit eight centuries and averaged over 100 in the Test series against Pakistan, but Middlesex slipped to thirteenth and mounted no real Championship challenge.

I did manage 110 wickets but the season for Middlesex was overshadowed by the death of Patsy Hendren at the age of 73. He was a brilliant batsman who was second only to Sir Jack Hobbs in the list of all-time century-makers with 170 hundreds to his name. So far as I was concerned, he was also a dry Londoner who had begun his Lord's career like me, selling scorecards at the ground. From 1952 to 1960, the keeper of the Middlesex scorebook was the man who scored more runs for the county than anyone else before or since, Elias 'Patsy' Hendren. I never saw him play, except on film, but I will always be delighted to have known him well in his last years when he stayed close to the game he loved by officially recording the successes and failures of his successors. The great thing about Patsy was that he never complained that cricket in his day had been any better or harder. Patsy was a wise and sensitive man who knew perfectly well that cricket becomes not better nor worse as the years go by, but simply different.

He also possessed a great knowledge of all the county grounds around the country, having played for Middlesex for several decades but, to be honest, his advice was not always helpful. After playing for several seasons at Old Trafford, we were surprised to find the fixture had been switched to Liverpool one year. We would always quiz Patsy as to what this unknown ground was like and he would invariably reply, 'Oh not bad, not bad. I got a hundred there once.' But as he racked up so many hundreds, this was not exactly helpful or surprising.

Patsy was also a great storyteller and practical joker. One of his favourite routines was to stagger along a railway station platform as if he were drunk just as the train was leaving and trying to wind up as many people as possible. He brightened the game for us in his later years as much as he did for all the crowds during his amazing career. Everyone at Lord's was desperately sad when he died.

1962 was also the year I got back into the England team, just seven years after my last international appearance. I knew this was a make or break year and, apart from my success against Cambridge, unfortunately I did not get off to a particularly good start. I did get in the wickets at Middlesbrough and Stroud during May, but it was not enough to earn me a place in the MCC game against the tourists.

In the summer, however, my luck turned and I was included in the England team for the third Test against Pakistan at Headingley. My friend Ken Barrington was the star of the show with a painstaking 119. I did not get much of a bowl, although I did chip in with 2 wickets for 3 runs in the first innings.

I was also delighted to be selected for the Gentlemen v Players match at Lord's a week later. With the MCC side to visit Australia due to be selected ten days afterwards, this match was very much a Test trial. Rev David Sheppard was widely tipped to be named as captain of the touring side and it seemed he had done his cause a great deal of good as he hit an excellent 112 before I managed to get him caught and bowled. But, in fact, Ted Dexter was named as captain. The Rev's wicket was the only one I claimed in that first innings and, when the Players went in to bat on the Thursday, the weather was heavy and oppressive. The conditions were ideal for Trevor Bailey and he bowled so well that he finished with figures of 6 for 58. But the Players captain Freddie Trueman and yours truly came together in the middle to stage something of a fightback. Freddie opened his formidable shoulders and crashed 2 giant sixes and 9 fours. I decided I had better get a move on as well, and hit 3 sixes and 7 fours and scored 70 in two hours before we were all out for 260. Parfitt and Edrich made a game effort at our run chase on the last day but the rain beat everyone in the end and the match finished in a draw. But it was most definitely a victory for me.

Afterwards, Walter Robins, who was chairman of the selectors, came up to me and said, 'What are you doing letting Trueman get all of the runs? You were just playing up and down.' I tried to explain that there was no batting to follow me. If I got out, that would have been the end. With just the hint of a twinkle in his eye, Mr Robins said to me, 'If your captain in Australia this winter tells you to get a move on, what will you do?'

I thought carefully, because they still hadn't picked the side at that point, and I decided to answer diplomatically that I would always bat as my captain instructed. 'If he tells me to hit out, I will hit out, Mr Robins.'

He smiled in approval. It was a generous and highly irregular gesture. He was letting me know before the touring party was announced that I was in it. On a good day, I can still recall the exhilarating lift it gave me.

5

BOWLING THEM OVER DOWN UNDER

On earlier tours to Australia, the MCC team would travel all the way by ship, but in 1962 the long sea voyage was shortened by flying to Aden and then sailing the rest of the way on board the luxurious liner *Canberra*. We stayed for two nights in Aden, and it was seven years since I had been there before on the ill-starred 'unofficial' tour of Pakistan. On that previous occasion, heavy rain had spoiled the visit, but this time the weather was kinder.

Our hosts were the Army and the RAF and they treated us like royalty. We were accommodated in the officers' mess and I got rather a different view of service life than I had experienced as an aircraftsman from 1951–53. We were taken for a trip around the harbour in a big, high-powered motor launch and then enjoyed a leisurely picnic on one of the beautiful beaches. It geared us up perfectly for the luxury that awaited us on board the *Canberra*. It was only the ship's second voyage and it was certainly a wonderful way to travel, especially as we were accommodated in first-class cabins. I shared with my pal John Murray and we soon got used to the formality of dressing for dinner every night. We settled down immediately to enjoy a relaxing 12-day cruise… unfortunately, our captain Ted Dexter had other ideas. And he had help.

Ted had discovered that Gordon Pirie, the Olympic distance runner, was on the ship, so he decided it would be a great idea to ask for his assistance in getting us extra fit. After a long season, many of us were enjoying the rest, so this development was not exactly welcomed with open arms. Gordon was quite keen on the plan, at least partly because he was travelling in third-class and Ted, who was very keen on physical fitness, got him instantly upgraded.

One of the reasons for flying us out as far as Aden was to shorten the length of the sea voyage as previous cricketing tourists had been known to lose what fitness they had when they boarded and put on a good deal of weight. With Pirie on board, there was not much chance of this happening. Personally, I didn't object too much as I always liked to try to keep myself fit; in fact, one of my proudest moments came when Pirie shouted at John Murray and I to slow down while we were having our daily sprint round the decks. Other members of our party were not so enthusiastic. Freddie Trueman is a wonderful cricketer and, in spite of his fearsome reputation, he is normally a relaxed and genial companion, but he was firmly of the opinion that the business of being one of the world's fastest and most consistent bowlers was more than enough exercise to keep him fit.

At first, Freddie developed a training technique of ducking across the *Canberra* through a corridor which ran more or less across the middle of the ship to lessen the strain of doing complete circuits. When that ruse was rumbled, Freddie took to the more simple expedient of simply lagging back a little. Pirie had just competed in an important athletics meeting when a leg injury had wrecked his chances of victory. At the best of times, he was not an easy guy to get on with and he made the mistake of picking on Freddie. Pirie shouted at Freddie that he was not trying and demanded more effort from his legs. Freddie fixed him with that famously formidable stare and said, 'Listen sunshine, these legs have bowled 1,400 f*****g overs this year and they haven't let me down once. I've never lost a final when it really mattered,' he added pointedly. 'If you don't shut up, you'll be going over the f*****g side.'

That sort of ended Pirie's training sessions and, when he got to Australia, he wrote an angry newspaper article criticising our attitude to his training methods and accusing us of being sloppy and unprofessional. We had just finished a long season in England, so it was a bit unfair.

When Pirie had finished with us, we brought out the slip cradles and had some fairly intense fielding practice.

This was important for keeping our hands hard and our reactions working quickly. In addition to the physical jerks, the cradle and the deck sports, we also had the daily chore of signing autographs. It was rather like having to do lines at school, except that you would have had to be an unusually badly-behaved pupil to be given 700 a day to do, which was what we were faced with. You would have to be a very self-absorbed person indeed to derive anything but finger-aching boredom from writing your own name and nothing else for an hour a day. I seem to recall that many of Freddie Trueman's were unfortunately blown out of a porthole – or, at least, that was his story!

The social life on board was pretty hectic. Hardly a day passed without a cocktail party. The captain gave one, then so did the first officer. So did some of the passengers. Naturally we felt bound to return the hospitality. One way and another, you can tell that the idea of a pleasant, relaxed voyage turned out to have been rather a pipe dream.

We also had to find time for the traditional one day fixture at Columbo. The Ceylonese, as they were then called, made us very welcome during our few hours ashore and, although we had been at sea for only a few days, it was a relief to stretch our legs on firm ground again. The climate was less of a relief after the air-conditioned first-class cabins. It was very hot and sticky and I remember David Larter leaving the field at the end of the day literally dripping wet.

The ground was packed with excited spectators. In

My childhood memories are mainly very happy and I was always very close to my sister Peggy. We got on well, whether we were on holiday at Southend (*above left*) and with our big brother Billy and our dad (*below left*), or at home in London (*above right*). And she really looked after me when we were evacuated to Rutland in 1939 (*below right*).

The Titmus family might not have had too much money but we always knew how to look our best.

Above left and right: Happy holidays.

Below left: Peg and I dressed to kill, with Billy towering over us.

Below right: Yours truly aged eleven.

Above: Mum and Dad on the beach at Southend.

Left: My first game for Middlesex, against Somerset in 1949 aged 16.

Above: London Play Centre Cup winners 1945-46. I'm second from the right on the front row, trying not to look too pleased with myself. Our coach Mr Snow recommended me for a trial with Chelsea Youth.

Below: Shaking hands with the Prince Philip with (*from left*) Mike Brearley, Peter Parfitt and John Price.

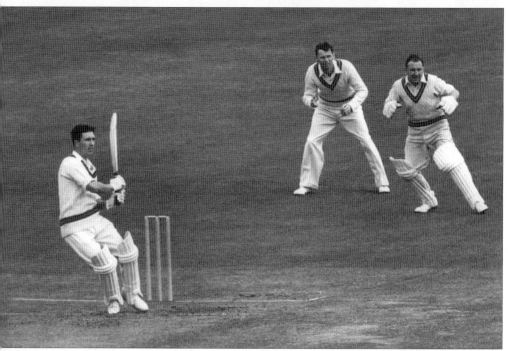

Above: Middlesex 1950. I might look like a boy among men (*back row, left*) but my new team-mates made me feel very welcome. *Back row, left to right*: Alec Thompson, Reg Routledge, Laurie Grey, Leslie Compton, Doug Newman, Harry Sharp. *Front row, left to right*: Jack Robertson, Jim Sims, Gubby Allen, Sid Brown, Jack Young.

Below: Happy hooking against Notts at Lord's.

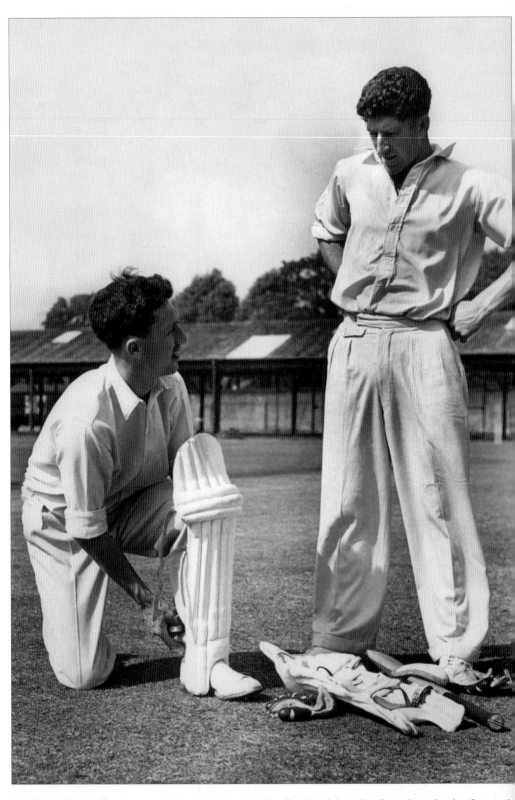

Ken Barrington looks on as I pad up to play for England for the first time, in the Second Test against South Africa in 1955. Ken made his debut in the First Test and we became great friends.

Cricket can seriously damage your health. A ball from Shackleton of Hampshire took my breath away (*above*) and another from Somerset's Lomax was equally painful.

Above: A chorus of Middlesex cheers herald a fine catch by John Murray to dismiss Mervyn Kitchen off Alan Moss.

Below: The first time three spinners were selected to face Australia. *From left*, captain Ted Dexter, David Allen, Ray Illingworth and me.

those days, they rarely saw a touring side and the expectation grew as we went in first to bat. David Sheppard delighted the crowd. He was bang on form and he scored 73 out of our 181 for 8 wickets declared. By the time we had to leave to get back on the boat, which was due to sail that evening, Ceylon had made 152 for 8, so honours were broadly even. They had one remarkable slogger, Gunasekara, who hit a sparkling 76. Evidently, he usually got runs and he was certainly a much better player than any we thought we'd face.

Back on board the *Canberra*, we continued our rigorous social and athletic life. John Murray and I had our own steward who helped us to dress for dinner every night. We had three highly enjoyable weeks on the boat. The steward got 'married' during the voyage and John and I were invited to the wedding. Seven o'clock every night he would be there waiting to brush the fluff off the shoulders of our dinner suits. At the end of the night, the boys would often come in and we'd have a few beers and a bit of a laugh and next morning the gay steward would come in and say, 'Oh, Mr Titmus and Mr Murray, you've done it again!' Somehow, the parties always seemed to be in our cabin.

The Duke of Norfolk, who was the manager for the tour, joined us at Columbo and commenced his official duties. He arrived with his three attractive daughters and he was frank in his introduction. 'You may dance with my daughters,' said the Duke with a beaming smile. 'You may take them out and wine them and dine them, but that is all you may do.' They were three very pleasant girls, but I am not sure that Colin Cowdrey actually heeded this advice as, some years later, he went on to marry one of them!

The Duke was clearly a man of the world and he was a success from the start. He was very friendly to the players and we felt that he was entirely on our side. He always tried to put us first, even when it meant ordering us not to hold so many parties in our rooms at Adelaide. The sight of the premier Duke of England standing half-naked shaving in the communal washrooms up country was a sight to behold.

The Australians took the Duke's appointment as a great compliment to themselves so he became a great social asset as well. But he was no soft touch. We received some fairly unpleasant criticism after one match when some chap stood up at a dinner to make a speech, whereupon he started insulting Brits in general and us in particular. The Duke had to respond and just stood up and said, 'Thank you very much for inviting us. We really have enjoyed ourselves. Good night.' And with that he led us out of the room. Jaws dropped all over the place but the Duke was not prepared to take any nonsense and the players really appreciated his leadership. He was not with us all the time as he had to fly home rather mysteriously around Christmas. He did get some flak for this at the time because we were all far from home ourselves, but it transpired years later that he had been asked to come home to help plan a state funeral. In any case, the Duke took a great deal of the burden of responsibility for leadership from the captain, Ted Dexter, and he helped greatly in dealing with the press.

While His Grace was back in the UK, the newly-appointed Secretary of the MCC, Billy Griffith, came out to take over. With Alec Bedser already in place as the Duke's very able assistant, this was one tour that was not going to suffer through lack of leadership.

A cricketer is never more in the public eye than when he is Australia and the captain is watched more closely than anyone else. The press never leave you alone from the moment you dock at Fremantle until the day after the final Test. In those days, thousands and thousands of words of analysis, praise and criticism were written, printed and flashed round the world. If you had a slight cold, then the symptoms would be quickly transmitted everywhere in the world that cricket is played. If you had the misfortune to put down a catch or fail at a crucial moment, the full details of your ignominy would be recorded in hundreds of newspaper reports.

On this particular tour, we arrived to the opening salvo from Gordon Pirie, who reacted to Freddie Trueman's comments by criticising the physical fitness of the MCC side. I felt this was below the belt. At any rate, John Murray and I agreed at the time that we had never been in better shape in our lives.

Selecting a touring side is a difficult task and whoever you choose you are going to be attacked for leaving this man out or putting that man in. The side with which I went to Australia was – with the possible exception of Lock for one of us spinners – the obvious one to choose. On their records at the time, Pullar and Sheppard were the best openers. The Rev had enjoyed a fairly good season and had made a century in what proved to be the last Gentlemen v Players match. Geoff Pullar was an experienced England opening bat already. He had a big-match temperament without doubt. The importance of the occasion never worried him.

As it turned out, that great Aussie bowler Alan Davidson came out on top. He worked out our openers more successfully than they worked him out. The pity was that we did not take a third regular opener with us. It is easy to see this with hindsight, but more difficult to suggest who might have been the correct candidate for the job. This perhaps proves the selectors right. If they had taken another opener then either Parfitt, Graveney, Barrington or Cowdrey would have had to have been omitted. Mike Stewart and John Edrich, the Surrey openers, had the best claim, but you couldn't say that it was more justified than that of the other four.

If Pullar had got on top of Davidson, the problem would not have arisen, but in the fifth Test, with the possibility of winning the Ashes still very much there, he was injured and Colin Cowdrey was sent in first in his place. Colin did not like opening and it affected the side badly when he did the job. When he batted at his favourite number four, you knew you still had Colin to come and this was very good for morale whenever you made a bad start. But Colin got three ducks in his first six innings in Australia. We had made our bad start and there was no Colin to come. I believe that to ask him to open was to sacrifice him and it would have been better to have sacrificed someone else. That was what happened in the second innings of the last Test when Ray Illingworth went in with David Sheppard. Then Colin came in later and scored 53, which surely proves my point.

It was fascinating to play with two great batsmen like Colin and Ted Dexter and to watch their different approaches to the game. Ted was only truly world-class when he was attacking. Then there was no one to touch him. When he was defending, he didn't measure up to Colin. That is not to say Ted did not play some useful defensive innings, but he was a man of impulse, a flamboyant character who could completely dominate the game when he was on the attack. Colin, on the other hand, could play some very fine innings even when he was not attacking. He was a more moody batsman than Ted. He could be tied down by the most ordinary bowling and made to look a very mediocre bat, but against fine bowling he seemed to grow in stature and he could look like the best player in the game.

But allowing for the undoubted genius of both Colin and Ted, the batsman I came to admire the most was Kenny Barrington. He was a true professional who had really worked out his batting. He took time to really work out his game. He learned what he could do and he learned to accept what he could not do. He had fantastic concentration and he really used to apply himself to the business of scoring runs. Kenny was often criticised for being slow and he was once told, 'I always switch off the television when you come in,' by a fellow passenger who recognised him on a train. He could be dull from the spectators' point of view, but I felt sorry for him that he was judged more on his slowness than on the number of runs he scored. With Dexter and Cowdrey and others to provide the more dazzling displays of batting, it was surely vital to have a Barrington in the side as a sheet anchor.

There was some criticism of Tom Graveney's inclusion in the side. He had been to Australia twice before without achieving too much success, although he hit a fine century in the fifth Test at Sydney in 1955. This was an innings that lasted long in many memories, although it happened after the Ashes had been won, so he never quite got all the credit for it that he might have done. In my experience, the Australians never let anyone get a century against them cheaply, so the fact that the series had been decided should not have been allowed to detract from Tom's performance. To me, then, he was an obvious choice to tour. His record against other countries was very good and there was every chance he would perform well.

Tom had been out of cricket in 1961 when the Australians were in England because he had left Gloucester and was qualifying for Worcester, but when he returned in 1962 he looked a far better player than ever before. Tom Graveney's Test career was a mystery that defied analysis, but I only know that I always had a very high regard for Tom as a batsman. He was one of the players on any wicket whom I least liked bowling to and he remains a close friend. I was thrilled when he became the first professional cricketer to be elected president of the MCC this year.

My other Middlesex chum Peter Parfitt had played some big innings in the series against Pakistan, but he was to have a disappointing tour. He made 80 at Brisbane but lost his place to Tom Graveney. In the state matches, he was asked to open and, because he can never turn down a challenge, he agreed; but it was not a success.

The batting did not end there. There were also our wicket-keepers John Murray and Alan Smith and the three all-rounders Barry Knight, Ray Illingworth and myself. I should perhaps include Freddie Trueman in this category, too, because he had some useful knocks in the Tests and the previous season in England he had been taking his batting very seriously indeed and had scored two centuries. Unfortunately, John Murray did not come off with the bat in Australia and Alan Smith was preferred to him in all but the third Test. John was then injured during the match which was very bad luck. John was the better keeper but we needed all the batting we could command.

If you look at the figures, I had the best tour of all the

all-rounders – and naturally I was looking at the figures! I had a good start which is so important in a tour of Australia. The preliminary matches are only a build up to the Tests. If you do well in the early games and get into the England team, then you are naturally given more opportunities. As it happened, the luck was with me and I got my place and kept it.

Barry Knight had a good preliminary tour as a batsman. He got a century against the Australian XI at Melbourne and fifties at Perth and Adelaide before that. He didn't get much opportunity with the ball. His batting carried him into the first Test but then his form deserted him. Ironically, he took three wickets in the first innings, his best bowling on the tour, but he lost his place and did not regain it. I think Barry's seam bowling was much more effective in England but he was a fine all-rounder.

Ray Illingworth had to wait until the fourth Test before he got in the side and he was not given a great deal to do on the tour. I always regarded Ray as one of the best all-rounders of my day. We met for the first time in the RAF where we played together and became friends. He thinks a lot about the game and plays it hard. Of course, because we both performed the same role we were rivals, but he suffered this time because he did not play well in the early games.

No one could accuse Ray Illingworth of being a 'fun' person exactly. If you asked him mid-season how it was going, he would rattle off exactly how many overs he had bowled for how many wickets, but small-talk was not his thing. David Allen of Gloucestershire was in the squad as the main spinner, but I forced my way into the Test side and stayed there. At the time of the first Test, it was true to say that the three spinners – Ray, myself and David Allen – were bowling equally well. But I had taken a few more wickets than they had and I had the edge on them with the bat. Anyway, I got in and they were left out.

The fast bowling was, of course, dominated by Freddie Trueman and Brian Statham. Freddie on form was the most dangerous bowler in the world at this time. He was very different from Brian, more unpredictable, and for that reason more exciting to watch. You never knew quite what to expect with Fred. One minute he would be magnificent and the next he would be struggling off his short run and becoming very frustrated and demonstrative.

With Brian you knew more or less where the ball would pitch and he was always a model of consistency. Brian was a run-up bowler and Fred was a power man. Both were great bowlers.

These were the players who arrived at Fremantle in October 1962 facing the considerable task of trying to recapture the Ashes.

Brisbane and my first Test against Australia were about 2,500 miles and seven weeks away when I got my first glimpse of the sub-continent. First, we stayed in Perth and got in a lot of practice in nets as good as any I have ever used. I was very lucky to make a good start in our first match against Western Australia. I collected three wickets in their first innings and two in their second. More important, though, was the 88 I scored in our first innings. I came in when we had lost six wickets for 161. Only Ted Dexter had performed well, and when Alan Smith joined me we were floundering. We put on 119 and, from a personal point of view, it was very good for the morale to start the tour with some runs. I even managed to hit a six and 7 fours. The fact that I continued to oblige in this department in the team-building weeks before the first Test certainly gave me the edge, I am sure, over the other spinners. Similarly, Alan Smith's success with the bat gave him an early advantage over the rival wicket-keeper, my pal John Murray.

In the Western Australia match, which we eventually won by ten wickets, the bowler who got me out was Tony Lock. He had been left out of the MCC touring party and had smartly accepted an invitation to play with the state team for the winter, and he eventually went on to settle in Australia permanently. I believe Tony should have been in our party. Apart from his bowling, he was a great fielder and we failed to win the series because of our fielding. He would also have benefited greatly from the large number of left-handers in the Australian team.

I was credited with bowling into the rough made by Fred Trueman's run through. This was nonsense, because I got most of my wickets in the first innings before Fred's rough was there. Anyhow, I also got right-handers out.

The rough did not help me but it would have helped Tony when he was faced by left-handers. They would have had to play him. Yet one can understand why the selectors did not choose Tony. He didn't have a particularly good season in England in 1962, and he had not shone on his previous tour of Australia with Peter May's team.

I was glad to be rested for the other big match at Perth because it was a game we eventually lost by ten wickets which was a big setback so early in the tour. It didn't help the morale of the team, either, when Tony Lock took 3 for 36 in our first innings, prompting the press immediately to question our chances of retaining the Ashes. It always seemed to come as a shock to journalists when a touring side loses to anything less than a full Test side. But it shouldn't be a surprise, especially in Australia. A state side usually includes more than a few international players; the Combined XI which we lost heavily to included top players like Lawry, Simpson, O'Neill, McKenzie, Sheppard and Tony Lock. Nonetheless, a ten-wicket defeat was dispiriting, but perhaps served as a timely wake-up call.

We flew into Adelaide for the next big match. Our hotel was on the seafront and the Adelaide Oval is one of the prettiest cricket grounds I have ever visited. It was an oasis of green in a dry and dusty city and the match against South Australia was a personal triumph for me as I scored 137 not out, the highest score of my career. Of course, the old image came searing back to life again. Crawford White was quick to refer to me as 'Little Fred

Titmus, the cheerful Cockney kid from Lord's'. I decided to take this as a happy omen and prepared to reduce myself to midget size all over again.

It was a beautiful wicket to bat on. The ball didn't spin very much and it never moved off the seam at all. If a slow bowler sent a short one down, you could almost pick your spot anywhere on the ground and place the ball there. Four wickets were down for 232 when I came in. Kenny Barrington had scored his century and Tom Graveney missed his by only one. I joined Kenny at the crease and he looked as if he was wilting a little under the conditions. He had been batting most of the day and, when I arrived, he said, 'Bloody hot, Fred. We'll cut out the short singles.'

I didn't think much of that idea and retorted, 'We'll cut out yours.'

It was a high-scoring match and I shared hundred partnerships with Barry Knight and Alan Smith. It was a batsman's paradise and I was delighted not to have muffed the chance of getting easy runs. Even so, not everyone admired my performance. One of their bowlers was moved to say crossly to me, 'The way you're batting, you might as well hold it upside down.'

Naturally, I made the only possible reply. 'The way you're bowling, I agree, I might just as well!'

Several of the papers commented on the fact that this was only the fourth century of my career and yet I had accumulated more than 12,000 first-class runs. One eager statistician dug up the fact that only seven other batsmen had scored over 10,000 runs and hit four or fewer centuries. In my case, and probably in the others also, the reason for this may have been because, when batting fairly low down the order, there isn't usually time to get to three figures. Or that may just be my excuse. Scoring a century was very good for my ego, though, despite the papers kept giving me credit for being modest.

The Adelaide match petered out in a draw, and so did the next game at Melbourne. This was another big-scoring game with Dexter, Barrington and Knight getting centuries and Colin Cowdrey coming back into form with 88. I scored 37 and we declared at over 600. I am sure this was the first time that the Australians recognised that we had any batting.

Melbourne looked almost English with all its Victorian-style buildings and we were made to feel more at home when we palled up with the stars of the *Black-and-White Minstrel Show* who were enjoying a successful run in town. They came to see us and we went to see them and it helped to make our stay a happy one.

The Australian XI at Melbourne included Neil Harvey. I managed to get him out in both innings but not before he had knocked up 51 in the first. It was Neil's last season and it was a shame that his amazing career should end in an uncharacteristic outburst of bad temper against Ted Dexter. I never did get to the bottom of the row but perhaps it was just because he and Ted were total opposites as people. All I know is that his press comments on Ted lost him a lot of friends. These attacks upset the MCC players more than anything else that happened on the tour, and for Neil to retire from the game on this sour note was disappointing for those who had played with and against him, and for the public who had enjoyed his performances. International cricket helps you see the world and gives you the opportunity of providing crowds with much pleasure. It is a great pity when you let personal spite spoil the good things. For all this, you couldn't help admiring some of Neil's knocks, including his sixth Test century against England. He was nearly always exciting to watch because he was the sort of batsman who was supremely capable of winning or saving a match. He was also good to bowl to because he gave you a chance; he played shots and he took risks. And his fielding was quite brilliant; in this series, it was easily the best on either side. He stopped some wonderful shots in the covers and took some terrific catches. It was just sad to see such a talented man consumed by such bitterness.

After two drawn games came another defeat. Once again, I was glad to be out of it. New South Wales beat us at Sydney by an innings and 80 runs which was fairly sensational. Kenny Barrington was also rested in that match and we took out our cameras together and went filming in the little seaside resorts which are a feature of the outlying suburbs of Sydney. We thought the world-famous Bondi Beach was rather disappointing and inferior to many beaches in England, but then Kenny and

I were great patriots and we were still happy to be at Bondi instead of watching our colleagues going down before the New South Wales attack.

While we were in Sydney, we became a little tired of hearing people singing the praises of their bridge, which is, of course, even more renowned than Bondi Beach. The Sydneyites were evidently obsessively proud of it and it is undoubtedly a fine piece of engineering and a spectacular sight. But when every other person you meet says, 'How do you like our bridge?' it is not surprising that Freddie Trueman was the first to lose patience. 'It ought to be all right...' said Freddie bluntly, ' ...it were made in Yorkshire.'

The four amateurs on the tour were Colin Cowdrey, Ted Dexter, Alan Smith and the Rev David Sheppard, and all their wives were brought out for the tour while our wives had to stay at home. We couldn't have afforded to take our wives to Australia but we weren't allowed to even if we'd had the money. They didn't come for the whole six months but they came for a good length of time. Susie Dexter was there for ages. She was a model and she had modelling jobs along the way. Freddie Trueman used to do his nut when he saw her attract all the press coverage. The air would really be blue when Freddie opened the paper and saw the beautiful Susie Dexter splashed all over the place. 'We're getting paid a pittance and how much is she getting paid?' Fred wanted to know.

There was a lot of grumbling but cricket was a completely different world back then. I didn't necessarily disagree with Fred, but the differences between amateurs and professionals never got me as wound up as it did him. I was just pleased to be touring Australia playing cricket.

Several times in Australia, I met people who claimed to be related to me. Having a more unusual name than many presumably accounts for this, but it was puzzling that a succession of total strangers would ring me at one of our hotels and announce he or she was my long-lost relative. Not having a very strongly-developed sense of family, I was not immediately overjoyed at these announcements, and when they didn't even know which branch of the family they were supposed to be related to, I became completely indifferent.

Kenny Barrington and I did not miss all of the New South Wales match. We were there for the last afternoon when the wicket broke up and anyone could have bowled a side out with an orange. This might not quite do justice to Richie Benaud, who took 7 for 18 in a great spell of bowling, but he did get Tom Graveney with a ball which hit a foot-hole and bounced back on to the wicket. The press gave us a lot of stick, even more than Bobbie Simpson and Norman O'Neill had when they put on 234 for the second wicket. This fairly comprehensive thrashing probably did us no harm and we went off to Brisbane determined to fight back.

We almost won the state match against Queensland where Wesley Hall, who opened the bowling, was no trouble at all. Every one of our batsmen played well, except me, and, in the Queensland first innings, so did most of them. In the second innings, however, Ted Dexter had a great spell and Tom Graveney even took a couple of wickets so that, by the close, they needed 54 runs to avert an innings defeat with only three wickets left standing.

Nevertheless, we were not exactly favourites when Lawry and Simpson walked out to face Trueman and Statham on the first morning of the first Test at Brisbane. The opening Test at Brisbane has a history of having important psychological effects on the teams. The four England teams before ours had all lost there. Even Len Hutton's eventually victorious side went down there by an innings. We drew the match and I believe this was the turning point of our tour. Nobody expected us to come out of it with our dignity and pride intact.

On the first morning, the wicket was very good but Freddie Trueman bowled with lots of fire and he got Bill Lawry and Norman O'Neill out early on. Freddie really had a go at the batsmen that morning, as he did several more times on that tour. He put in a great deal of effort and every now and then he clicked and bowled with perfect rhythm, and this was one of those occasions. We knew that if Norman O'Neill got set in, he would be difficult to shift. We found that, in order to get him out, you had to get him out early. When he first came in, he was nervous, so our policy was to keep the bowling tight and attack him.

That morning, Freddie got him early with the score at

only 46 but then, gradually, the Aussies began to build a decent score. At the end, Richie Benaud and Ken Mackay were still there and the score was 321 for 7. My first Test wicket of the tour came late in the day when Brian Booth, who had by then moved smoothly on to 112, stepped down the wicket to drive and mis-hit the ball to Ted Dexter who was fielding at mid-on. Brian Booth became something of a special victim of mine during the series. I got him out five times in eight innings, but it was a pity that I sometimes did not get him out more quickly, because he scored more runs against us than anyone else. He was a very good off-side player, so I used to bowl at the middle stump or middle-and-leg to try to tie him down.

It worked a couple of times, as at Brisbane, when he had a dart at me and I had him. We usually put five men on the leg side to bottle him up but, as his eventual aggregate of 404 runs showed, it did not work as effectively as all that. However, one has to think of what he might have scored if we had not used these tactics.

Australia were all out in that first innings for exactly the same number of runs as Booth scored in the series. We made a pretty good fist of matching them with 389. Ted Dexter hit a stylish 70; Ken Barrington worked away to 78; and my county pal Peter Parfitt chipped in with an excellent 80. I made a nervy 21 before Bobbie Simpson caught me off Richie Benaud.

The Australian second innings swept to a very comfortable 362 for 4 before Benaud declared. At the start of that last day, the Australian captain did not declare until just before play was due to begin. We needed 377 to win and Richie had not really left either side enough time to force a finish. But Geoff Pullar and David Sheppard made a solid start and, at lunch, they were both still there with 86 on the board. We had a discussion and thought we still stood an outside chance of a surprise win. By tea, we had changed our minds because the score had crept to only 185 and we could hardly expect to make 196 in two hours, even with Ted Dexter still in and looking for runs. At the close, Barry Knight and I were still there with 100 needed. Benaud had made it practically impossible for us to win, or for them. But who could blame him? You don't give away victory in a Test match, yet I think he could have chanced his arm a bit more on this occasion because the wicket was definitely wearing towards the end. On the fourth day, one of my jobs was to contain the Australian batting, and had I been able to bowl a little slower and give the ball more air, I think I might have had a fair number of wickets. Instead, I got one for too many runs.

This was a match dominated by batsmen. No fewer than 14 fifties were recorded in the four innings. It would be ridiculous to give the impression that Richie Benaud was an over-cautious person all the time. Like all Australians, he started off going all out to win. The caution only came in when things went wrong, and then he would shut the game up if he could. His own performances in this series were not remarkable. He did not do very well with the bat and his 17 wickets cost him 40 runs apiece. I thought he had lost some of his fire as a leg-break bowler. In England, he had bowled quicker and seemed to be at you the whole time. Over there, he gave the ball a little more air and lost a certain amount of zip.

Alan Davidson led their attack in this and other Tests. He had a beautiful action, run-up and delivery and, besides being pretty fast, he made the ball swing into the batsmen very late. Often, our batsmen had to make a hurried stroke against him because they thought it would not swing. Then when they got used to the fact that it did, he would send one down that didn't! But we found that the great thing about Alan was to keep him from getting a wicket in his first four or five overs. If this happened, he was inclined to lose enthusiasm and with it went his fire. Unfortunately for us, this seldom happened.

Then there were Ken Mackay, Peter Burge and Barry Jarman. Ken was in and out of the side during this series and I felt he had gone downhill a bit. In England, his great value was as a bowler of in-swingers or cutters. In Australia, he was regarded more as a batsman and he was a very difficult man to get out. But, like Peter Burge, he was made something of a scapegoat after their defeat at Melbourne. Ken was a most pleasant person and, although he may not have won his country a lot of Tests, he saved them from defeat on a few occasions.

Burge also went out of the side early on. He had done well in England in 1961 and he played competently enough at Brisbane. In the second Test, he failed to perform; he batted with great uncertainty and had a couple of sweeps at me, and then I got him leg before. Peter was not seen again until the final Test when he made a century in one innings and a not out 50 in the other, so the fact that he was dropped was quite lucky for us. Barry Jarman, the wicket-keeper at Brisbane, did not see the series out either. Wally Grout took over at Adelaide, but Barry was a very solid sort of stumper who never let them down.

6

MAKING THE
HEADLINES

After that first Test, the rest of the party journeyed to Townsville, while Kenny Barrington and I went straight to Melbourne. There we were happy to get to know a cricket-loving Yorkshire businessman called Jack Dews. He offered us one of his cars and suggested we took it for a spin. Kenny and I were more than a little surprised when we went round to the garage and the chauffeur handed us the keys to a shining new Bentley.

For once, my friend Kenny lost his nerve. He could drive everything from a tank to a scooter but the responsibility of being at the wheel of someone else's Bentley was too much for him. He drove along – rather as if he was in one of those back-to-the-wall innings he became so famous for – at about 20mph. When the strain got too much for him, he steered the car into a drive-in cinema and we sat there feeling rather grand watching a film from the comfort of 'our' Bentley. We also managed some golf at the Royal Melbourne Golf Club, so our visit was largely enjoyable.

Before the Melbourne Test, we had two more matches to fit in. Our colleagues beat Victoria by five wickets and then we went off to Adelaide to play South Australia again over the Christmas holiday. It was at Adelaide that one of our players escaped a large fine on the highly doubtful grounds of 'diplomatic immunity'. He was driving down the splendid new Anzac Highway when he opened up the engine and really let it rip. He realised he was being raced by another car and put his foot down even harder; only then did it become clear that he was being chased by the police! He was let off as soon as he identified himself and, shortly afterwards, a very similar thing happened to another player. I could not claim that it was right or fair for us to be treated in this privileged way but, occasionally at least, it can be very helpful to be sportsman.

Once again, the Adelaide Oval wicket played easily. Colin Cowdrey celebrated with 307 as several of the boys got runs. I took 3 for 88 and Kenny, who had a fair amount of bowling to do on this tour, also came off with 3 for 55.

When we flew back to Melbourne to renew the Test series, there was a clear feeling of confidence running through our team. The Melbourne Test was one of the hardest matches I have ever played in. When I was a young schoolboy back in London, and an England cricket team was touring Australia, I would get up early in the morning like thousands of others to listen to the Test match commentaries from the other side of the world. Still heavy with sleep and yawning, I would tune in to the ball-by-ball description of the game. There was nothing unusual in this, of course, but I had never expected ever to be sitting in the England dressing room at Melbourne years later doing the very same thing! The tension of the match was simply so unbearable that, at times, I could not go out on to the balcony and watch my team-mates batting. And this was not simply because I was a comparative newcomer to international cricket. My reaction was mirrored in others around me. Experienced players like Tom Graveney and Brian Statham sat at the radio with me, eager to know what was happening but far too involved in it to be able to bear seeing each ball bowled. This does not happen very often in my experience but, in this particular Test, the game swung so constantly from one side's favour to the other's that for those of us who were a living part of it, but not actually on the field at the time, the only way of not becoming over-excited was not to look!

On the first day, Australia made a good start. Lawry and Simpson put on 62 for the first wicket. When Alan Smith caught Simpson off Len Coldwell, Norman O'Neill came in and stayed with Bill Lawry until the score reached 111.

Now 111 is known among cricketers as 'Nelson', because there was the mistaken belief that Nelson had one eye, one arm and one leg; in fact, he had two legs. When 111 is reached, superstition has it that wickets are supposed to fall and, to avoid the bad luck associated with the number, the batting team off the pitch (and umpire David Shepherd) take their feet off the ground, or stand on one leg until more runs are scored. I don't know how far statisticians might prove this to be correct – probably they don't – but it is a very widely-held belief.

On this occasion at Melbourne, the curse of 111 struck again. Freddie Trueman bowled Lawry and one run later Coldwell had Neil Harvey for a duck. Then, at the same score, Brian Statham got rid of O'Neill, caught by Tom Graveney for a duck. Suddenly we were on top, but Peter Burge and Brian Booth put a stop to the rout and the game swung back in Australia's favour slightly. Then, dramatically, it went our way again. I was bowling and each batsmen played a couple of peculiar shots with the result that I had two quick wickets and we found ourselves in the ascendancy.

After that, there was another Australian stand between Davidson and Mackay. They put on 73 together and Ken showed just how difficult he could be to remove when the wicket was good. But half-an-hour before the close, Freddie Trueman got Davidson and the day ended with Australia on 263 for 7.

The next day, we took the new ball but Benaud and Mackay went steadily on. Forty minutes passed and I was put on again. Richie swept at me and Kenny Barrington took a splendid catch at deep square leg. Five runs later, Mackay tried a sweep, too, and I had him lbw. Trueman polished off McKenzie and Australia, who had at least twice looked set for a huge total, were all out for 316.

Our innings started badly. The Rev David Sheppard was out lbw to Davidson without scoring, and 19 runs later Geoff Pullar was bowled. All of a sudden, there was no doubt now who was on top... but not for long. Colin Cowdrey and Ted Dexter spent most of the rest of the day at the crease. Ted was attacking in his most brutally elegant form and looking totally in command. Colin was also at the top of his game, carving out his innings with the most brilliant shots and appearing to have all the time in the world to play them. The score raced on to 194 before Ted was caught by Simpson off Benaud and Kenny Barrington came in to join Colin and play out time.

The third day began well for us. Colin and Kenny added 60 runs before Colin was caught at square leg by Burge. Kenny was leg before in the next over and the very good lead we had all been looking forward to started to appear very doubtful indeed. When the seventh wicket fell, we were still one short of the Australian total but we finally scrambled to 331, just 15 runs in front. With the knowledge that we would have to bat last on a crumbling pitch, it did not seem a big enough lead.

The odds were slightly in favour of Australia when Lawry and Simpson walked out to open their second innings. But the gods were on Freddie Trueman's side. He bowled magnificently, better even with the second new ball than with the first. By the end of the day, Freddie had sent back Simpson and O'Neill but, at the close, Lawry was still there and Brian Booth had just joined him.

Just before lunch on the fourth day they were still together, doggedly adding slowly but surely to the score. Ted put himself on and, with the last ball before the interval, he kept one low and bowled Lawry to break the stand. That made them 161 for 5.

We felt we were favourites again in this see-saw match but, before we could return to the attack, play was interrupted by drizzle. When play resumed, Booth and Alan Davidson shared a stubborn stand which I managed to break when I got one to turn and Davidson was caught behind the wicket. Then Freddie Trueman took over with the second new ball. It was mid-afternoon and very hot, but Freddie ignored the conditions and rushed in and bowled brilliantly. He had Mackay lbw and Benaud beautifully caught by Cowdrey at slip. Freddie grinned to himself and bowled McKenzie and that was that. We had a day-and-a-half to make 234.

But nothing is easy in Test match cricket. We had another bad start. Geoff Pullar was out to a magnificent catch by stumper Barry Jarman off McKenzie with only five on the board, but Ted and David Sheppard stayed there until bad light put a stop to proceedings. The last day was the one we spent by the radio. Now 225 runs might not sound very much for an England side to score in a whole day with nine wickets still standing, but it was the fifth day and there was every likelihood of the wicket breaking up. The fortunes of the match had already changed so rapidly that victory by any reasonable margin, if at all, seemed more than anyone dared hope for. As we sat, trying not to expect too much, listening to the commentators, the score mounted confidently and, at lunch, the two Sussex men were still there with the total at 96.

After lunch, it continued in much the same way until I ventured none too bravely on to the balcony only to see David Sheppard judge a call badly and Ted was run out. Immediately, the tension returned to the game. Colin Cowdrey had done well in the first innings so, by the law of averages, there was a good chance that he would not do so well this time round. He did, though, and he was still there when the Rev ran himself out trying to make the winning hit. Victory soon followed and we switched off the radio.

Looking at the score sheet all these years later, it appears that England won easily. In fact, we got home by seven wickets. But even on the last day, it was a struggle and, if we had lost a couple of quick wickets, we might well have been defeated. It was this continual swing of fortune that made Melbourne so memorable to me, and why I remember it as the hardest Test match I ever played in. It was the first Test match that England had won in Australia since 1955.

After that excitement, it was a relief to go to Tasmania for a couple of matches with the pressure off. We even had time for a fishing trip, which was followed by a barbecue on a lonely stretch of beach. This outing had its amusing side when the genial commentator Brian Johnston fell out of the boat with all his clothes on. I even had my camera at the ready and took a photograph. Brian always liked a joke, so he was quick to see the funny side. Then, it was back to Sydney for the third Test and it was a match that began brightly but ended badly.

We batted first and Colin Cowdrey shone again. Freddie Trueman and I had a 50 stand for the eighth wicket and we each finished with 32. When they went in, I had a good day and got among the wickets and had a 4 for 5 spell which gave the press a field day with headlines like 'LITTLE FRED COCKS A KING-SIZE COCKNEY SNOOK' and 'TITMUS THE LITTLE MAN WHO WAS ALWAYS THERE'. 'BOY TITMUS COMES OF AGE' said the *Sydney Daily Telegraph* and dug out an old photograph of me going out to bat in that first match at Bath in 1949. The *Sun-Herald* called me the 'perky little Cockney wrecker'. Well, it was all very flattering and I won't pretend not to have been pleased, even if they did harp on a bit about me being so little. I ended with 7 for 79 and the Aussies were only 40 runs ahead. It was a very good spell and I was told afterwards that it was the first time an Englishman had taken 7 wickets for 16 years. I managed to get the Aussies tied down for once and in one spell of eight, eight-ball overs, I dismissed Harvey, Simpson, O'Neill and Booth for only five runs.

The crowd at Sydney was always very vocal and I enjoyed fielding just in front of the famous Hill. The banter was flying around and I kept it going with a wave and a cheery grin or two. They were very patriotic, of course, but always very good-natured. That was the time I was attracted by one particular Aussie who kept bellowing, 'Hey, Fred ... over here.' Eventually, I picked out the face in the crowd and it was the actor Ray Barrett. He was a big cricket fan who had often visited us at Lord's when he was working in England, so it was good to see him in his own patch, even if he was cheering for us to lose.

With a bit of luck, I felt we were heading for another victory but our second innings totalled only 104 and a great opportunity was lost. I really felt for my friend John Murray. It was his big chance and he injured his shoulder in the first innings leaping to catch Bill Lawry off Len Coldwell, and Peter Parfitt had had to keep wicket.

The good thing about the wicket at Sydney at that time was that it turned, although it was a little slow. The Aussies always seemed vulnerable to off-breaks when the pitch was turning and that day the wicket was just doing enough. You had to up your pace a little bit on slow pitches, which some spinners couldn't do. I was a medium-pacer at one time, so I could do that.

There was a wind blowing in the right direction at me and I had a bit of luck early on. On good days, like that day, impossible catches are made. Physically, it was not that tiring; it was hot, certainly, but spin bowling is not that tiring if you're fit. You can certainly do it for an hour or so or as long as you're getting wickets, and I never felt tired when I was taking wickets. If you got in the groove, you just wanted to keep going. Sometimes, Ted would take you off just as you thought you were really getting somewhere and it could be frustrating.

Bowling is always so much more preferable to fielding. I'd rather bowl than field any day. I never liked being just a fielder. I spent lot of time at second slip when the quick bowlers were on which I quite enjoyed until I dropped a catch or two. I remember the seven-wicket day very well. They had some very good players. John Murray got injured so I had Peter Parfitt keeping wicket.

John tore his ligaments quite badly and it was just downright bad luck that it should happen then. In the second innings, he had to bat because we were in trouble. They strapped him up and the poor bloke had to play one-handed. Alan Davidson and Graham Mackenzie were the leading Aussie pace bowlers of the day. John managed to stay around a bit and they took the new ball. It was an indication of the level of sportsmanship in those days that John batted for 94 minutes and not once did the ball bounce above waist high. They were very decent. Today, I am sure you would get two balls and if you were still around they would be whistling around your ears. Not once did they try to do anything other than bowl him out. It wasn't like that in those days. There would be the odd expletive exchanged between the sides occasionally, perhaps if you edged them for four, but cricket was played in a good spirit. There was nothing soft about the way we played, though; missiles would be flying around. And there was nothing soft about the competition. But at the end of the day, we would have a beer together. We never drank a lot, though, as we never had the money.

After that match, we lost our supremacy. We shared the honours in the fourth Test at Adelaide where I got my first Test 50 and had another successful end-of-innings stand with Trueman. I finished on 59 not out and was very pleased with myself. The press headlined us as 'THE FEARLESS FREDS' and 'THE FIGHTING FREDS', which made us sound like a music hall act. Mind you, with Freddie Trueman you were never short of entertainment.

The Aussies had scored 393 thanks largely to a huge stand between Neil Harvey and Norman O'Neill and, after some of our main batsmen had failed to distinguish themselves, we were left in the mire. I tried to bat sensibly and inched a few runs on to the board in small stands with Illingworth and Smith, but they were both out fairly cheaply, and in came Freddie Trueman who appeared determined to knock the cover off the ball. He blasted some very quick runs, which included two straight sixes off the mortified Richie Benaud. Freddie can always be counted on to surprise you. After the first towering six, he appealed against the light! Even for fiery Freddie, that was cheek of the highest order. Richie and I both burst out laughing and, needless to say, the appeal was not upheld. Test cricket can have its lighter moments. Freddie's response was to crash another giant six about 20 yards deeper but, unfortunately, he tried to do it again and was caught by Benaud off Mackay at extra cover. But we managed to get up to 331 and I finished on 59 not out. It wasn't pretty but it was effective and it helped us to avoid losing a close match which was eventually drawn.

Freddie's sense of humour kept us all laughing on many occasions. Sometimes, it seemed, he was so sharp he was in danger of cutting himself. When poor David Sheppard missed a catch, he instantly apologised to Fred: 'Sorry, Fred, I should have kept my hands together.'

'Nay, Reverend, thy mother's legs,' came the deadpan reply.

Freddie was always a great storyteller and he had perfected his own version of the Biblical tale of David and Goliath. It was extremely vulgar and studded with swear words, of course, but delivered by Freddie it was always hilariously funny. The Rev listened with what must have been growing horror the first time Freddie came out with it but, by the end, he was laughing as much as anyone. David Sheppard was a good bloke who could take a joke with the rest of them and he and Freddie became firm friends.

We had some very good laughs on tour. One night, a young lady knocked on David's door during the evening. He answered it and she apologised for bothering him, saying she was looking for Colin Cowdrey. Being a gentleman, David took it upon himself to escort this young girl along the corridor towards Colin's room, just as a group of players were coming the other way. It was all entirely innocent, I am sure, but the Rev David Sheppard took a great deal of ribbing over that.

Adelaide was a very sociable town and some players drew attention to themselves by enjoying a drink or two in their rooms after the match. We were celebrating Len Coldwell's birthday and it was all fairly innocent. Evidently, one or two other guests found the noise level a shade irritating and complained. Naturally, it only lasted for a moment or so, but the whole non-event was immediately whipped up by the newspapers. The Duke of Norfolk was pushed into getting involved and banned parties in hotel rooms for the rest of the tour, but perhaps the last word on the matter should be left to the hotel manager, Mr Charles Weston. He said the party had gone on rather late but that the team would always be welcome at his hotel.

Had the press picked up another incident I might have got a less flattering nickname. After the Sydney Test, we had been up-country for a day away from cricket and on our way back we stopped at a fish and chip shop. There was a nice little touch of home about the place. Just as the woman was about to slap the fish and chips on to the opened newspaper, one of the boys said, 'Don't throw it in his face, lady!' The paper was open at a large photo of me. I could so easily have been dubbed 'FISH FACE' after that, or I suppose it would have been 'LITTLE FISH FACE'.

Before the final Test back at Sydney, we went up to Canberra for a one-day game against the Prime Minister's XI. These one-day games were enjoyable because they had a festival air about them. We liked them especially when the other side batted first so that we could go in after tea and try to knock off the runs quickly. The two-day games, however, were taken more seriously but they were really a waste of time from a cricket point of view. The wickets we played on were good, and some of the players opposing us were very useful, but their whole object was to make sure they didn't lose to the MCC touring side, so the cricket was not very interesting and there was never time to force a decision. From a financial angle, I am sure the one-day games were as good as the two-day matches so there was a message there for the future.

At Canberra, a great feature of the match was that Sir Donald Bradman and Alec Bedser turned out. Many of us had never seen the Don play, let alone played against him, so this should have been a thrilling occasion, but as so often when the greats of the past come out of retirement, he failed. He scored only four and everyone was very disappointed. In a way, it was just as well, as I had planned to take a cine film of the innings. I recorded him coming out of the pavilion but then my film ran out!

I loved touring. It was wonderful to see foreign countries and be able to meet people like Sir Donald Bradman, who had been my hero when I was a boy. I am 5 foot 9 inches and I reckon Don was a couple of inches smaller. I was surprised that he was not taller, but it only makes his achievements all the more remarkable. He was a tough little man. I never saw him bat in a Test match live because, when the Aussies came in 1948, I couldn't afford to go. But I have seen film of him playing and he has got to be the most natural player there has ever been. He was interesting to talk to and he was quite a good golfer, too. I enjoyed a round with Don, who was charming company. I went with Alec Bedser to his home in Sydney once for dinner. Alec had got him out more than anybody but he still thought he was the greatest player who had ever lived. Alec and Eric continued to visit Don in Australia until just before he died in 2001.

While we were at Canberra, we were entertained by Sir Robert Menzies, the Prime Minister. He was a great cricket fan and came to a number of our matches. Cricketers are never over-fond of official dinners but, somehow, Sir Robert always made his functions enjoyable and this time he made a kind gesture towards Freddie Trueman. On discovering that it was Freddie's birthday, he had a silver tankard inscribed for the occasion. It was pretty thoughtful, but I'm not sure Freddie was so delighted as he always insisted his reputation as a big drinker was unfair. I think he had a point.

Freddie Trueman and Brian Statham, or 'George' as we used to call him, were a great pair, but they were like chalk and cheese. Freddie was always full of life and fun, while George was quiet and self-contained. Freddie used to grumble that he had this reputation as a bit of a drinker, while George was seen as the model professional. In fact, Freddie never drank very heavily. He talked a lot, and he was always ready with a story or two, but he was never a big drinker. He would get a pint of beer early in the evening and it would last him for ages. I never saw Freddie drunk. George, on the other hand, would sit knocking back the drinks pretty steadily at the end of the day before going quietly off to his room, and it never seemed to affect him. That left us to return to Sydney for the decisive fifth Test. England needed to win the match to regain the Ashes but caution was always the order of the day and the result was an inevitable and disappointing draw. We opened with a first innings total of 321, thanks largely to a fairly sedate century from Kenny Barrington. I managed 34 runs, but there was a feeling that it was all happening too slowly.

The Aussies made 349 runs in reply and I had some success with the ball, finishing with figures of 5 for 103 from 47.2 eight ball overs. Ted Dexter was widely criticised after declaring our second innings at 268 for 8 at lunchtime, leaving the home side to get 240 runs to win in the time remaining. It was a challenge Richie Benaud did not wish to accept.

He had warned earlier that he had no intention of throwing away the Ashes by accepting a challenge that amounted to a 'juvenile dare' and he was as cautious as his word. The crowd booed, barracked and slow-handclapped but the Australians refused to try for a result. It was disappointing but, somehow, inevitable. Winning or losing the Ashes was even then such a huge event that no captain wanted to take unnecessary risks.

Because Australia already held the Ashes, they held on to

them as the series was drawn. Ted Dexter claimed afterwards that the spectre of the greatest prize in cricket was what had really spoiled what should have been a stirring climax to an enthralling series. Ted went further and suggested the historic Ashes should be scrapped. He said, 'If there had been no Ashes and £1,000 a man for winning today's game, I daresay there would have been a result. The fact that these matches are played in a series is a damper. The fact that the Ashes must be fought for is a further damper. I believe that if a series is drawn, then the Ashes should at least go into pawn so that no one holds them.'

On this tour, the two captains, Ted Dexter and Richie Benaud, were lined up to face press conferences after each day's play during the Tests. Both of them were later criticised for failing to make the series more interesting to the public but, in my opinion, neither of them should have been blamed. Each of them was right in refusing to throw away the series. The press blamed them for drawing it, but just think how either of them would have been carved up if he had deliberately risked losing it. Richie Benaud particularly took the view that if he could not win, then he would make sure he did not lose; that is why he took no chances on declarations. Richie was a good captain for Australia and he did go all out to win but, if they got into a mess, his team could play as defensively as any other. When Benaud's men were up against it, they set their sights on a draw, and although this may have been dull for the spectators, I believe it is the only way Test cricket can be played.

Richie Benaud eventually blamed the lack of a final winner on the 'ascendancy of ball over bat' which seemed an odd thought to me. I had thoroughly enjoyed the series and, while I agreed with Ted that the fear of losing the Ashes had been a strong influence on causing cautious cricket, I could not in my heart criticise Richie for doing everything he could to avoid losing.

I was delighted to finish fourth in the batting averages and as our leading Test wicket taker. Freddie Trueman took 20 Test wickets and I managed to get 21. I think I remembered to remind Freddie of those figures once or twice before we got home.

We went on to play three Tests against New Zealand in a post script to the series that made sure we did not return to England until late March. After the excitement of Australia, it was a little tame in the cricketing sense but it was very pleasant to have a glimpse of the two beautiful islands. In the four matches we played, most of us did well and the Tests were won comfortably.

The climate was agreeable except when we were in Dunedin, where it was very cold. I went out to bat wearing my pyjama trousers underneath my flannels, which is a trick I can certainly recommend! One pleasure of that trip was to find a genuine long-lost relation – my uncle had emigrated to New Zealand in the 1920s and lost touch. In Auckland, I met his family for the first time and it was a happy reunion before the long trip home.

7

THE WINDIES
STORM IN

After being away in Australia for almost six months, it took some time to get back down to earth for the 1963 county cricket season. The arguments over the Ashes and the cautious approaches of both sides went on for a while, but I still had to pinch myself to make sure I was not dreaming. Playing five Test matches against the Aussies – then, as now, the ultimate cricketing opponents – was a fantastic experience. We had drawn the series and I had enjoyed enough personal high points to dare to feel reasonably happy with my performances.

I felt so sorry, though, for my friends John Murray and Peter Parfitt. John had injured his shoulder at a crucial time and Peter had been forced into the unfamiliar position of opener that had not helped his tour. I knew they would both come good again and I will always

FRED TITMUS – MY LIFE IN CRICKET

remember how generous they were in congratulating me on my comparative good fortune. Without wishing to become too sentimental, the greatest thing I got from cricket was good friends, and John and Peter remain, to this day, two of the best.

There were certainly times during 1963 when it felt as if I had hardly played any cricket at all. An awful lot of days were lost to rain as the English weather did its worst and my time with Middlesex was interrupted by Test calls for the series against the West Indies. So I found myself playing fewer innings than at any time since the summer of 1954, and I bowled fewer overs as well. Consequently, I failed in my attempts to do the 'double', although at the end of August I thought I still had a good chance, needing only 127 runs and 17 wickets. I got nine more victims in the Surrey match and there were two games to play. The Derbyshire fixture at Lord's was almost completely washed out, however and, at Southampton, where I was part of an MCC All-England team sent down to play the county on the occasion of its centenary, I had my last chance. I got the wickets but I fell short on the runs.

Despite one of the worst summers in several years, there was probably more interest in cricket than at any time since 1953, when England first regained the Ashes after the war. The West Indians captured the public imagination and their own supporters lined up in droves to cheer them on and shout continuous advice. The newly-instituted knockout competition also drew crowds, particularly to

Hove, where Sussex knocked out Yorkshire, and to Lord's in September, where Sussex were again victorious in the Final.

I appreciated the boost in interest cricket received from limited overs competition, but I always wished that more people would turn up to see the exciting finishes of some of the county matches.

My benefit match at Lord's against Sussex at the start of June built to a terrific climax. Sussex set us a target of 112 and over two hours to get them in, which could hardly have been more entertaining for the crowd. In the end, we were beaten by one run with only a few minutes to go. What more could you want from a cricket match than that? Yet there was only a sparse, third-day crowd present. Not that I had any complaints about the support as a whole. On the Saturday and Monday they turned up in good numbers and contributed generously to my gate. But I think the tension of the match might have got to my England skipper at one point. So far as I can recall, no one has actually sworn at me on the cricket field, although Ted Dexter, the opposing captain in my benefit match in 1963, did mutter something that sounded uncomplimentary when I made an unsuccessful lbw appeal against him. But one can put that down to friendly badinage, I hope! When I went in to bat, I was certainly expecting to be given the traditional one off the mark. No one wants to get a duck in their own benefit match. But Ted was bowling when I went in and he said, 'If you think you're getting a free hit from me, you are very much mistaken, Titmus!' That was typical Ted.

Benefits are much more elaborately organised affairs these days but, in 1963, I was very grateful to the large numbers of people who helped to make mine a success. The wives and non-playing members arranged teas and sold scorecards and their efforts were enormous and entirely voluntary. These splendid people always rise to the occasion and, in my case, we were unusually lucky because we had mostly fine Sundays and my benefit fund was greatly increased.

Spurs footballers Peter Baker, Terry Dyson, Bobbie Smith and Tony Marchi played in a match at my home club Enfield, and I remember centre-forward Smith took a magnificent catch. Ian Carmichael, the actor, played in two of the other matches, along with Michael Cray, Tony Mercer from the Black-and-White Minstrels, Don Charles, Sam Kidd and Colin Welland. It also helped swell the crowd when Freddie Trueman turned up on the Sunday of the Middlesex v Yorkshire match. That was a very friendly gesture I'll never forget.

But the real cricketing attraction of the summer of 1963 were the West Indies tourists. The first representative game, as always, was the MCC fixture at Lord's in late May. This was the first time that the real bowling force of the tourists was seen. You might say it was the first time that the combination of Hall and Griffith really hit us. And they were to go on hitting us all summer, as Brian Close would have been the first to testify.

To face sheer speed and aggression of the like generated

by Wesley Hall and Charlie Griffith was quite an ordeal for batsmen. And the onslaught is harder to take when the only alternatives are the wiles of Gary Sobers and Lance Gibbs. It was in the MCC match that we learned what a good bowler Gibbs really was, particularly on a wicket that was helping him a bit. It was dusty but otherwise not especially favourable to him, so his success was even more to his credit. At that time, he was comfortably the best off-spinner in the world. His length, direction and variation of pace were all excellent and he had very good flight, helped by his long hands and fingers. Of course, he was helped by coming on after Hall and Griffith. When the two fearsome pacemen were rested, the batsmen often felt they could relax and hit the ball about. But then came Gibbs and the great Gary Sobers with his enormous ability and versatility.

As a bowler, I did not get much of an insight into the batting of the West Indians. The wicket was still fairly good while I was on. I got 3 for 50-odd and didn't bowl too badly, but I can't say I saw my way to working them out. To be honest, I am not sure that you could work them out in the same was as you could the Australians. The West Indies were so inventive and naturally talented that they were hard to predict in any phase of the game. And they had Rohan Kanhai, a remarkable batsman in my view. I found him very hard even to set a field to, as you never knew how he was going to play. One day he would stride in and play immaculately straight up and down the line, and another he would walk out and start hitting you all over the place.

On this occasion, we also had an introduction to Conrad Hunte, who looked a terrific player. I felt he was going to be possibly the best opener in the world after this match. He was a beautiful stroke-player on both sides of the wicket and had a very sound forward and backward defence. He hit the ball as hard as any of his colleagues, which is very hard indeed and, unlike some of them, he did not seem to get fed up or lose patience.

As we approached the first Test at Old Trafford, it was clear England faced a serious challenge. As it turned out, it was clear that the toss was going to be crucial and they won it and swept away for a day-and-a-half on a good batting wicket. The ball came into the bat, it didn't bounce a lot, and it didn't deviate off the seam very much… and it most certainly did not spin.

Hunte scored 182, Kanhai 90, Sobers 64 and Frankie Worrell 74 not out. They reached 501 for the loss of only 6 wickets and declared. I bowled 40 overs for 105 runs and a single wicket – it was not my happiest day by any means. Kanhai was like Denis Compton, a complete law unto himself. The situation of the game never seemed to determine how he was going to play. His direction seemed to come from within himself. He was a man of moods who played attacking strokes with what sometimes appeared to be a reckless abandon but usually with great success. He really made hay on that wicket and, by the morning of the second day, we could see the wicket starting to turn; we knew that if our goose was not exactly cooked, it was already being slipped into the oven.

Mickey Stewart and John Edrich did manage to get us off to a reasonable start, but it was disturbing to note that Wes Hall got the first three wickets on a pitch not, for once, made for seamers. But this was no help phsychologically when facing a total of 501. The wicket got worse and harder and the ball started to bounce so Gibbs, who can exploit this situation very well, ended with 5 for 59. Griffith bowled steadily in this innings but he never looked dangerous and it was Wes Hall who looked much more like being the spearhead of the attack during the series. Ted Dexter tried to launch a fight back and did hammer 103 runs himself, but we were all out for 205 and forced to follow-on.

Second time around, Mickey and John were extra determined and they did put on 93 for the first wicket. We were still a long way behind but we thought it was just possible, if we could get 120 or so ahead, that we might get them out cheaply. Some hope! Gibbs conjured up 6 more wickets and we reached 296. We had levelled the scores and David Allen was required to bowl just one ball to give them the run they needed for victory.

The second Test at Lord's is the match that has been talked about perhaps more than any other in my time. I believe it has now rightly gone down as one of the greatest matches of all time. It was played in the teeth of rain, wind and bad light and it ended just as dramatically as is possible, with both sides within an ace of winning. For many years, people in the Middlesex side had been saying that if you wanted to win a Test match at Lord's, you should include Derek Shackleton in the England side. This happened for the first time when Brian Statham was dropped in his favour for the second contest with the mighty West Indies. The theory from players in our team was that the wicket at Lord's was grassy and the ball moved about off the seam for medium bowlers – but not necessarily for fast ones. The theory did not prove entirely correct on this memorable occasion because, although Derek did well and got 7 wickets in the match, Freddie Trueman did better and got 11.

Once again, the West Indies won the toss and decided to bat. They put on 51 runs for the first wicket but here the figures lied, I felt. At lunch on the first day, they could easily have been 60 for 6 because Trueman and Shackleton beat the bat so many times that it seemed amazing to us on the field that the scorecard as we came off should be reading 50 for none. I was fielding at cover or mid-wicket at this time, close enough to see what was going on, and certainly close enough to watch the anguished reactions of the wicket-keeper and the slips. Kanhai played one of his more subdued innings on this occasion and got 73.

Solomon chipped in with 56. Joe Solomon was one of those cricketers who doesn't get noticed that much but he had a knack of doing well in awkward situations so he was always a good man to have on your side.

I was not surprised that Ted did not call on me to bowl in the first innings. David Allen bowled a few overs but was not very successful, and Freddie and Derek were doing pretty well between them. In fact, Derek ended the innings on a real personal high note by taking the last three wickets in four balls. West Indies finished on 301 with what we thought was a fair amount of good fortune.

We were poised to hit back and, not for the first time, Ted Dexter elected to lead from the front. We had a disastrous start, with Charlie Griffith blasting out both openers very cheaply and Ted unleashing one of the finest displays of controlled aggression I have ever witnessed. His 70 was electrifying. He stood up and hit the quick bowlers all over the show for an hour. Ted obviously said to himself, 'This is me or you,' and set about it, hitting hard and fast but never slogging wildly. Unusually for me, I watched a large part of this innings and I remember one particularly magnificent drive off the back foot past extra cover off Hall and a tremendous hook off Griffith. It was the longest I have ever witnessed Ted bat because I have this superstitious feeling that if I continue to watch, he will get out. Despite the fact that I always loved playing, I was never the greatest watcher of cricket.

By the end of the day, I was in and the wicket was playing fairly well. Jim Parks was with me but he went before the close and, on Saturday, there seemed a reasonable chance that we might end up with a first innings lead. In the end, we failed by just four runs. I had a bit of a stand with Freddie Trueman and then another shorter one with Derek Shackleton for the last wicket.

The wicket was still fairly good. The bowlers tended to go for my leg stump but I kept getting twos and threes and pushing the score along. With the new ball due, however, there was little hope of turning the last wicket stand into a big partnership and, when Derek was bowled by Charlie Griffith, I was left with an unbeaten 52 to my credit.

By lunchtime, we had already hit back and taken two West Indies wickets and, if Butcher had not come in and made a point of staying, we might have won easily. I discovered that I had certainly underestimated Basil Butcher's abilities when I first saw him. His stance and grip seemed unusual and he made a little bit of a flourish when he lifted up his bat, but the runs he got in this series, and the way he got them, quickly altered my opinion. That day, he and Frankie Worrell put on 100 together just when the bigger-name batsmen appeared to be faltering.

Freddie and Derek bowled well, but Ted was off the field with the knee injury that used to trouble him from time to time. Colin Cowdrey acted as skipper and, with no Ted to call on, David Allen and I were given some overs. David got a wicket but I didn't.

Unlike some of my friends in the press, I saw no reason why I should have been put on because, when the seam bowlers are getting wickets in a Test match as closely contested as this one, there is no point in risking the spinners. If Ted had not been injured, I would probably not have bowled at all, but the fast men needed a rest.

An amazing collapse took place on the Monday morning. West Indies were 214 for 5 at the end of Saturday. The five remaining wickets went for only 15 runs when we resumed. The West Indies were all out for 229 and Trueman and Shackleton had put us right back in the match.

Monday was a grim, dark day with rain clouds always threatening. But for the weather, a finish would have seemed likely by nightfall. We lost 3 quick wickets for 31 runs, but Colin Cowdrey suddenly seemed to be playing the ball really well for the first time in the series. He was really timing it beautifully in that wonderfully unhurried style that could win any match when catastrophe struck. Colin was on 19 when he got a short delivery from Wes Hall which really lifted. To protect himself, he put his arm up and the ball broke it. After a minute or two, he knew he could not continue and walked off, very disappointed, knowing he was unlikely to take any further part in the game. Of course, as it turned out, he was quite wrong about that.

Brian Close joined Kenny Barrington in the middle. Kenny responded to the crisis by hitting a couple of tremendous sixes into the grandstand off a somewhat chastened Lancelot Gibbs. Like all of Kenny's batting, this was a calculated move. The fast men had come off for a break and the light was getting worse. We needed to get runs while we could and the chance might not occur again for a while. They came off two or three times for bad light and then the rain set in as soon as the Queen and the Duke of Edinburgh arrived. It was soon evident that any decision on this agonisingly poised match would have to wait until Tuesday.

Unfortunately for us, Kenny did not stay around long on the Tuesday. He had contributed a very valuable 60 runs when he was caught by wicket-keeper Murray, bowled Griffith. Tuesday was another sombre, rain-threatening day which was to be seized with both hands by the bravery of one Brian Close. This was the day when the uncompromising Yorkshireman put his body literally on the line for his country. He finished it black-and-blue with bruises as he stopped the ball with his body whenever it did not seem safe to play a stroke. Once or twice, he ventured down the wicket to Wes Hall, an exercise you might say, in counter-intimidation. It certainly surprised the bowler, there is no doubt about that.

The first time it happened, he stopped short in mid-delivery and it looked for a moment as if he had strained his back. Frankie Worrell was reported as saying afterwards that Brian threw the game away, but he did not say that at all. What he did say was that Brian had played a magnificent innings, but that he couldn't see why he had played particular shots at particular balls. And it was probably something he was half-muttering when he was undoing his boots, anyway. Mind you, it was also said of Worrell himself at this stage of the match that he was quite unworried. Obviously, the commentators did not have their binoculars trained on him too carefully because, when I came out to bat, just before tea, Frankie's face was most definitely betraying a great deal of tension, which was not entirely surprising.

I scored a quiet 11 and, while I was in, I always felt that we were going to win the match. Neither Brian nor I seemed to be in any trouble until I got a ball from Wes Hall which was slower than I anticipated. I pushed at it harder than I should have done and got snapped up at forward short-leg by McMorris. Unfortunately for me, he was standing deep enough to see it. If he had been a bit closer in, which was his usual position, I think it would have gone through.

Just to add to the excitement, Freddie Trueman was caught at the wicket first ball and then it seemed we were doomed to lose. But Brian hung on with David Allen's gallant support. The score moved slowly on, not quite keeping pace with the clock. The tension was much too much for me to watch and I went for a shower and a rub down.

Next, Brian was out, also caught at the wicket. Brian got 70 very valuable runs with his do-or-die technique before he was out. And with just two balls to go, Derek Shackleton was run out. At this stage, the crowd did not know whether or not Colin would come back to resume his innings. When he did, a huge roar of approval ran round the ground. Fortunately, the batsmen had crossed and David Allen had the strike. Six was needed to win the match and the ground was encircled by a baying crowd encroaching nearer and nearer to the field of play. Anything could happen – David might be out; he might hit a six and win the game; he might take a single, followed by an overthrow for four, resulting in a tie; Wes Hall might be no-balled; there might suddenly be a cloudburst. The situation could not have been more perfect for a thrilling finish.

In fact, David took no chances, successfully withstood the last ball, the crowd swept on to the pitch, the players fought their way into the pavilion and, a few minutes later, the heavens opened.

The remaining three Test matches could never quite match that for excitement, but they did all end decisively. At Edgbaston, we won surprisingly easily on the last afternoon after nearly five days of play interrupted by rain. England brought in Peter Richardson for John Edrich, Tony Lock for David Allen and Philip Sharpe for Cowdrey, who was to spend the rest of the series with his arm in a sling, watching from the television commentator's box.

We batted first and scored only 216. Sobers bowled very well and the ball moved in the air quite a lot. He got 5 wickets for 60, while Hall and Griffith were surprisingly ineffective for once. They were unable to make the ball swing late, which is what Sobers did to great effect to get his wickets.

The conditions were ideal for seamers and Trueman and Shackleton came out on top. Trueman was magnificent and, in the second innings, he bowled as quickly as anyone in the series. From the slips, where I was fielding, I could tell that the ball was hitting Parks's gloves harder and higher than any other bowler. There was no need for me to bowl in this game and I was not invited to. Tony Lock had to bowl only two overs, but came into his own as a batsman in our second innings when he made his first Test 50 in a partnership of 89 for the ninth wicket with Phil Sharpe.

Ted Dexter also bowled extremely well in this match but it was Freddie Trueman's performance after lunch on the last day which was the real highlight of the match. His last six wickets were taken in a 24-ball spell which cost him just one scoring stroke, a four from Lance Gibbs. He found a beautiful rhythm and made the ball swing, ensuring us a most decisive victory by 217 runs, which left the series even with two matches to play.

For the Leeds match, Peter Richardson was dropped and Brian Bolus came in. This was another game in which we would have done a lot better if we had won the toss, and I think we would have exploited the wicket more than they did. As it was, our batting was pretty inexcusable because, although the wicket did get worse, it did not deteriorate as quickly as all that. The West Indies certainly took advantage of the good batting wicket on the first day and punished the bad ball. Unfortunately, this was one of those days when my length was varied. We were surprised that Tony Lock was not put on until late in the day, but that was the captain's privilege and Ted Dexter chose not to share his thoughts with the rest of us. When Tony did get a bowl, he got Sobers just after he reached his century and Kanhai just before he arrived at the magic 100. Considering their scores at the time, they may both have been suffering some sort of mental relapse, but Tony still got the wickets. The West Indies finished on 397, which looked even more impressive after we had been bowled out for 174.

For once, all of our batsmen failed and we were 93 for 8 when Tony Lock joined me in the middle and we put on 79 together. I got 33, which was second-top score to Tony's flashing 53.

Charlie Griffith was the man who did the most damage to our innings. He took 6 for 36 on what was not really a fast bowler's wicket. He bowled very well and his bouncers were on a length from which you had to protect yourself. They didn't go over your head so you had to take a chance. I think we lost this match because we batted badly as a team in the first innings.

They began their second innings well, throwing their bats at everything, even though they lost their openers cheaply. Fortunately, when I got a bowl, Kanhai was already out and Sobers and Solomon were together. This was the one innings of the series when I got some wickets, including that of Frankie Worrell for a duck, caught behind by Jim Parks. This was the only time that Jim, who had replaced Keith Andrew after Old Trafford, had to keep to the slow bowlers for any length of time. It is always easier to keep to fast, rather than slow, bowlers, but Jim did not let us down. It was known that he was played in this rubber more for his batting than for his wicketkeeping and, in our second innings at Leeds, he did his best to stave of defeat with a gallant 57. But, by then, the wicket was turning and I don't think we were ever likely to get the 450-odd we needed to win. Even the rain let us down and, when I think how often it interfered with Middlesex's chance of victory that summer, it is odd that it never seemed to get in the West Indies' way.

At The Oval, it was my turn to be dropped from the original 12 selected. From what I saw of the first two days' play while I was twelfth man, I was not unduly disappointed at being left out, even though I believed is was unwise for an international side to go into the field with only one recognised spinner for a game that would last over six days. The wicket was almost certain to wear, although, in this case, I may have been proved wrong, because I am told it was still playing easily on the fourth day.

By then, I was down at Worcester and enjoying what seemed at the time to be the rare privilege of having a long spell of bowling. I had 12 wickets in the match on the ground where I have taken more wickets than any other ground but Lord's. And during the eight days from Saturday to Saturday inclusive, I accumulated 31 victims, which helped me clinch 100 for the season. I might well have been left out of the Test team, because it was common knowledge that the ball does swing at The Oval, or because it was thought that, in the event of the West Indians getting on top, an extra seam-bowler would be useful for keeping runs down. I certainly don't think I would have got many wickets there but I did fancy what I saw of the pitch as a batsman. I also had the transitory satisfaction of people saying, 'They should never have left you out.' But had it been Tony Lock or Derek Shackleton who'd been dropped, no doubt they would have been told exactly the same thing. England lost the match with only Philip Sharpe doing really well with the bat, which was all the more surprising considering the poor form he had been showing for his county.

The public's imagination really was captured by the image of these two fine fast bowlers Wesley Hall and Charlie Griffith. Wes was a tearaway bowler with a long run who seemed to bowl as fast as he could all the time. Charlie was the power house who did not seem to need or use a particularly quick run up. Griffith never seemed to be affected by the wicket. It didn't matter to his yorker, nor to his shorter ball that hit you in the ribs like a cannonball or whistled past your head. He was both fast and accurate and, a lot of the time, it was just a question of defending yourself against him.

During the Middlesex v West Indies game later in the season, Joe Solomon needed help from the crowd to remind his skipper of his abilities. A fan in the open stands was rooting for Joe loudly and kept shouting, 'Put Solomon on.' Worrell took the advice and took 3 for 23, including the valuable wicket of Peter Parfitt as he was moving steadily towards his century.

Sadly, 1963 was not a great year for Middlesex. The county finished sixth in the Championship as Colin Drybrough took over the captaincy from Ian Bedford, who retired from the game. This was the year when the distinction between amateur and professional cricketers was officially expunged. But social differences are never wiped out by a simple rule change and, in any case, traditions died hard at my county. The appointment of Drybrough as skipper, who was an Oxford Blue amateur, and very much from the old school, could hardly be said to have been moving with the times. Unfortunately for him, he was not a very good captain, either. The batting was not good enough that year, even though Parfitt, White, Eric Russell and Hooker passed the 1,000 run mark, and I might have done if it had not been for Test calls. The good news was that a young pace- bowler called John Price burst on to the county scene. He played in all of the Championship matches and took 80 wickets at 22.21, a performance which earned him a place alongside yours truly on the MCC tour to India that winter.

8

CAPTAIN'S INNINGS

Slow bowlers are vital in India, but even on pitches which did not especially help the spinners on England's tour of 1964, I managed to take 27 wickets in the series – almost twice as many as any other spinner on either side. Mind you, I bowled almost 400 overs during that series. It was a huge workload, but it had its rewards. Not that I got off to a very bright start. I had a boil on my spinning finger just before the tour started and I put a plaster on to avoid getting an infection. When we gathered in Bombay for a wonderful reception at the home of the Deputy High Commissioner, this plaster attracted quite a bit of press attention but the boil was fully healed by the time the cricket got serious.

I enjoyed my personal passage to India that winter, even though all five Test matches were inconclusively drawn.

There was still some excellent cricket played, even though dysentery did seem a more alarming foe than the Indian national side.

In Madras, we got off to a bad start by losing a crucial toss. The Indians batted and amassed 457 for 7 wickets before they decided to declare. I had some success and bowled 50 overs and took 5 wickets for 116 runs. It was hard work, but I thoroughly enjoyed myself, particularly when I trapped the formidable Nawab of Pataudi lbw for a duck. Perhaps it was better to play in than to watch, as I also managed eight successive maidens which did not exactly bring the crowd to its feet. And if they thought that was dull, then RG Nadkarni went on to bowl some 23 consecutive maidens, which established a new first-class record. My match figures were 9 for 162, having contributed to a very difficult match that finished in a draw after a real backs-to-the-wall rearguard action.

We lost Mickey Stewart and Jim Parks, who both went down with stomach upsets, and many of the rest of us felt a lot less than 100 per cent. Barry Knight and I both had to have drugs during the match to be able to stay on the field. I have to confess, I felt terrible, but I managed to take the first five wickets, and there's nothing like a little success with the ball to make you feel better.

In the second Test match at Bombay, we were suffering from a growing casualty list. Kenny Barrington had to pull out of the tour with a broken finger. John Edrich, Philip Sharpe and John Mortimore pulled out of the match with stomach disorders, and Mickey Stewart pulled out of the match with dysentery at tea on the first day and took no further part in the tour. In fact, we were so short of players that, at one stage, we seriously considered picking journalist Henry Blofeld, who had played at Eton and Cambridge. What a wonderful time the Dear Old Thing would have had recalling his Test début in Bombay. I'm not even sure he knew how close he came to it. Many of us were quite disappointed that Henry was not brought in to replace Mickey. We were left with a ten-man team comprising two specialist batsmen, two wicket-keepers, four fast-medium bowlers and two spinners, and somehow we managed not to lose, which was quite an achievement.

India scored 300 runs in their first innings and our makeshift team hit back with a scrambled 233. I'm proud to say I contributed 84 not out, my highest Test score, after five hours at the crease. This was one of those matches where Mike Smith showed really great leadership qualities in keeping our morale up in the face of a fiery crowd, who hurled bottles, and even shrivelled skulls, on to the pitch. The 40,000 spectators were remarkable. They stood and cheered and waved all day as if they were watching a Wembley FA Cup Final. We had a few people sick in hospital and I felt I was batting for them that day. It was particularly pleasing for me because Middlesex colleague John Price and I started the fightback together. Skipper Mike Smith had me blushing when he started talking about 'Fred's magnificent knock'.

John Price joined me for a stand that lasted for 143 minutes. He scored 32, which beat his previous best first-class score by 13. After he was out, Jeff Jones stayed in for 103 minutes, which was a tremendous effort. He only scored five but he gave me fantastic support until he was eventually run out, more through sheer exhaustion than miscalculation. It was a proud day, and I enjoyed every tense minute of it.

We somehow restricted their second innings to 249 before they declared, hoping to bowl us out. But Brian Bolus and Jimmy Binks led a tremendous second innings battle and the Indians could only claim three wickets. The match was drawn, according to all the record books, but it felt like a moral victory to us.

I was cheered to hear that Colin Cowdrey and Peter Parfitt were flying out from England as much needed replacements. This was great news for England in general, and me in particular, but it was very bad news for a young Indian bearer called Nanji with whom Peter Parfitt was anxious to renew acquaintance. On a previous tour, Nanji had packed all of Peter's gear up for the return trip but lots of bits and pieces seemed to get lost. Back in England, Peter had been furious and totally impotent. But, on his return, he was delighted to find in Bombay's vast accommodation section at the cricket ground that the very same Nanji was still employed. Naturally, he went in search of him and I'll never forget the look on Nanji's face when he saw the man whose gear he had lost

With Stephanie in Perth, 1974.

Above: John Murray leads the way in training around the deck of the *Canberra*. Athlete Gordon Pirie is second and Titmus third.

Below: The Duchess of York's charity golf day was a lot of fun.

Above: A family line-up. From the right it's yours truly, my son Mark, daughter Dawn, wife Stephanie, daughter Tandy and Tandy's partner Richard.

Below: Three generations of Titmuses. *From right*, my daughter Dawn, proud granddad and my daughter Tandy holding Dawn's baby daughter Charlotte.

Above: With my sister Peggy in Margate, 1998.

Below: Editorial conference to finalise this book. *From left*, my somewhat solid-looking ghost writer Stafford, his wife Janet, Tandy, Stephanie, yours truly.

Above: My wife Stephanie with our friends in Majorca, legendary Cala Bona tenor Joaquin Garcia and his wife Jackie.

Below: Cricket-loving Prime Minister John Major with Stephanie and me in 1992 at Paul Getty's cricket ground at Wormsley.

Above: Three spinners with more than 7,500 wickets between them were guests at the House of Commons. Don Shepherd (2,218), myself (2,830) and Derek Underwood (2,465).

Below: My 70th birthday party brought some old friends together again. *Back row from left:* Harry Latchman, Clive Radley, John Price, Don Bennett, Ron Hooker, John Murray Brian Hall. *Front row:* Peter Parfitt, Bob Gale and Frank Russell, the founder of the Cricketers' Club of London.

and heard Peter bellow, 'Nanji! Parfitt's back. Nanji! Parfitt's back!'

As far as the cricket was concerned, we had a splendid spirit in the side. Personally, I was delighted to be called up to bowl so much. In the first two Tests, one of the journalists was quick to confide that I had batted for 7 1/2 hours and bowled for almost 18 hours. A slightly too fulsome tribute to my performances concluded, 'Sobers is the greatest all-rounder in world cricket today, but, in a struggle for life, my choice would be battling Fred, the man who never gives up.' I most certainly would not like to play cricket for anyone's life, but I had to concede it was a kind thought.

We moved on to Calcutta, where we should have capitalised on a small first-innings lead, but rain reduced the time on the pitch and we produced another draw.

In Delhi, the batsmen ruled the day with the Nawab of Pataudi scoring a double-century as bowlers struggled in the heat to take wickets and the result was yet another draw. I had a 3 for 20 spell with the ball, but that proved a false dawn.

It was the same sad story in Kanpur for the fifth as unlucky Mike Smith lost his fifth consecutive toss. We scored 559, with yours truly contributing just 5 of them, but we didn't come close to bowling out the Indians. The averages showed I did well on the tour, which pleased me. I took 26 wickets in the series, which was apparently three short of the best bag in India by any visiting bowler.

Davidson and Benaud had each taken 29 and I can only say that, afterwards, they must have been very tired. Sadly, of the ten games on the tour, all but one finished in a draw. Clearly, if you prefer your cricket matches to come with definite results, then India is not the place for you.

After the tour of India, I had Middlesex's centenary season to look forward to, but unfortunately the results of the campaign gave little extra cause for celebration. After another poor start, we rallied a little to finish sixth. We did not manage to win at Lord's until we beat Leicestershire by 130 runs halfway through July. The batting still seemed very strong, with Eric Russell having a great year. He scored 2,050 runs in Championship matches alone and that was the first time anyone had managed that for a while.

Cricket can be an unpredictable game. After turning up at Nottingham for the First Test against Australia, I suddenly found myself being asked to open the innings – and with Geoff Boycott, no less, playing in his first Test. Just before play was due to start, opener John Edrich was declared unfit, having twisted an ankle in practice and, with no specialist batsman in reserve, I was invited to face the new ball.

I lasted for an hour to make 16 and survived a run-out after I had been knocked flat after colliding heavily with Hawke, the bowler, in the process of going for a run. I think he tripped me up deliberately but, of course, I'm biased. The ball was thrown to wicket-keeper Wally Grout and I was left completely stranded. But Wally simply held the ball and did nothing and allowed me to reach the crease and complete the run. 'Hurry up, Fred,' he said laconically. It was a great act of sportsmanship, but it did not seem that momentous at the time. In today's Test match arena, I imagine it would be something of a sensation. Wally and I became good friends and we exchanged blazers after that game.

In the second innings, I opened with Ted Dexter as Boycott had cracked a finger. I made 17 runs the second time around in a rain-ruined game that finished in a draw.

The Second Test at Lord's was drawn as well, as half the playing time was lost to rain. In the Third Test at Leeds, we batted first and scored a fairly moderate 268. But when they followed, they slumped to 187 for 7 and we seemed to have them pretty well tied down. At one point, I bowled 29 overs non-stop to take 3 for 27. But Ted Dexter decided to take the new ball and the runs started to flow. Peter Burge moved from 38 to 160 and they finished on 389. In all, I bowled 50 overs in that first innings to take 4 for 69. They bowled us out for 229 and then knocked off the 111 they needed to win pretty easily and beat us by 7 wickets. I don't like to criticise captains with the unfair benefit of hindsight too often, but Ted got things pretty wrong that day, I'm afraid. And it was the only match of the Test series to produce a conclusive result, so Australia retained the Ashes.

The Fifth Test at The Oval saw Freddie Trueman become the first bowler to take his 300th wicket, when he had Hawke caught by Cowdrey at slip. I was fielding at cover and I moved quickly to congratulate my friend. It was a fantastic achievement and I knew what effort had gone into it but, to be frank, I have to confess that I wanted to make sure that I was on all the newspaper photographs and television coverage of this historic moment. This match also saw Kenny Barrington score his 4,000th Test run and Colin Cowdrey his 5,000th.

I had a brilliant August with the ball. I took 7 for 70 against Surrey, 6 for 42 against Worcestershire, 9 for 57 against Lancashire and 7 for 73 against Derbyshire. I couldn't explain it, everything just started going right in one of those great pieces of form that makes bowling the greatest fun in the world. But we didn't win all of those games and it was clear that change was in the air.

As the 1964 season drew to a close, it became clear we would have a new captain for 1965. I was surprised to discover that it was going to be me. Democracy is all very well, but my experience is that, when a decision needs taking in county cricket, it sometimes needs a quick burst of dictatorship. Walter Robins was also the man who stepped in when we had a problem with the captaincy at Middlesex. Colin Drybrough was a very nice chap but, as a captain, I thought he was a joke. I also thought the county needed a change of leadership, but no one appeared to be doing anything about it until Mr Robins took John Murray and me out to dinner one evening. We were senior professionals at the time and he said he needed a private chat.

We were chatting when he stopped us for a second and said, 'Look, lads. We're having dinner together... call me Walter.'

John looked at me and we were both quite shocked. Respect was very important to me and I knew I couldn't do it and said, 'Mr Robins... the day I call you "Walter" will be the day I call the Queen "Elizabeth". I am sorry, sir. It is not going to happen.'

Once the ground rules were re-established, we got on with the business of the meeting, which was a change at the top. Colin Drybrough, the ex-Oxford University man whose leadership had been heavily criticised for most of his two years in charge, was apparently going to announce that he could no longer play regularly because of 'business commitments'. Evidently, I was the man Mr Robins had decided should take over the job and that was that.

I think it happened at the right time for me. I always used to say that I never opened my mouth for the first three years that I was in the Middlesex side because I was so young and so in awe of the senior players. Others used to say that I made up for it afterwards. By the time the announcement was made, I was on tour with the MCC in South Africa.

I was delighted to go because I love the country and I had a pretty good tour. Mike Smith was a fine skipper and I managed to finish among the wickets. Unfortunately, I also managed to finish in the headlines as well, thanks to a controversial slip of the tongue.

We set off in fine form and won three games in our opening two weeks. We even hammered Eastern Province, who included Graeme and Peter Pollock in their line up, by an innings and 150 runs in Port Elizabeth. I finished with match figures of 10 wickets for 70 and the *Daily Mirror* went overboard in their praise: 'Titmus has as much sorcery in his right hand as Stanley Matthews in his feet,' wrote their cricket reporter, which even I thought was pushing it a little.

We won the first Test in Durban pretty comfortably as well, by an innings and 104 runs. England ran up 485 with Ken Barrington and Jim Parks both hitting centuries, before declaring for the loss of only five wickets. Then we bowled the South Africans out cheaply twice. I took 5 for 66 and it was a very pleasing win because it was England's first victory in 12 consecutive Tests, the longest sequence without a success until then and not a record anyone wanted to maintain. Kenny's century made him the first player to reach 100 in all 7 of the countries then playing Test matches. It was a fabulous achievement by a man I was always very proud to call a friend.

He scored another in the Second Test at Johannesburg as we made the South Africans follow on again before rain and bad light forced the match to a draw. In the third Test, I was in trouble for calling their opener Eddie Barlow a 'cheating bastard'. It was just one of those things you can't plan for. I was bowling when he touched a ball with his bat and it was caught in the slips. Everyone knew he was out – with the unfortunate exception of the umpires – and it was so obvious he should have walked. I was annoyed and I let slip what I thought was a pretty accurate description. But Eddie was annoyed and walked down the wicket towards me with his bat raised. Bob Barber defused the incident. He just said, 'Calm down, Eddie, you're not big enough to start hitting anybody.' And Eddie calmed down. I was annoyed because he was definitely out and he knew it. Walking would have been the sporting thing to do.

After that, he went on to make 138, but we didn't clap his century, which made things worse. And just in case the South Africans needed a lesson in sportsmanship, Kenny Barrington walked after being given not out on 49. He knew he had touched a ball from Peter Pollock to wicket-keeper Lindsay, so he went. Kenny always was a very straight and uncomplicated guy. He knew it was the right thing to do, so he did it.

The match petered out into another draw and, at the end of the day, Mike Smith apologised for the 'uncomplimentary' words I had used. I was ordered to apologise, which I did the next morning. I just went into their dressing room and said, 'My captain says I have to apologise, so I'm apologising,' and walked off as quickly as possible. I think I let them know pretty clearly that I wasn't remotely sorry for anything. Mike Smith then tried to paper over the incident and pretend relations between the two teams were fine.

Eddie took it all in good part later and we had a laugh about it afterwards. Eddie was a bloody good cricketer but he was out that day and he carried on batting. Walking was quite a big thing. At county level, if you knew you were out, you walked. It was part of the game. If you didn't walk and the umpire didn't give you out and then found out that you should have gone, then the next time you were on a hiding to nothing. You walked because you knew the umpires would be after you. There weren't many in England who didn't walk and everybody knew who they were, so they were much more likely to be given out than you were. The level of appealing was not quite as hysterical in those days. And if you over-appeal, some umpires would have a quiet word and tell you that you weren't doing yourself any favours.

But all work and no play never did anyone any good. I've always been a keen golfer and I was delighted when journalist friend Ian Wooldridge invited me to join him in a round of golf with Gary Player. I think Gary was world number one at the time and Ian's article was to be about his experience as the world's worst golfer taking on the world's best. I was asked along to make up the numbers, but it was still an unforgettable day.

Gary Player was a lot kinder than I thought. Early on in our round, I hit my ball from an awkward position up on to the green. I couldn't see it land and I thought I had hit it much too hard. Imagine my delight when I arrived on the green to find my ball only six inches from the hole.

'Fred,' said Gary Player. 'That was one of the greatest golf shots I have ever seen.'

'Well, you won't want me to putt it then, will you?' And I picked it up and walked on. It was only later that Ian explained that Player had caught the ball as it was flying past and placed it by the hole to make me look good. He's been my favourite golfer ever since.

There was more controversy back at Johannesburg for the fourth Test. England elected to field in South Africa for the first time in 25 years and the home side swept to 390 for 6 declared in a rain-affected match. In England's first innings, their leg slip Van der Merwe threw down the wicket after the ball was tossed to him by the wicket-keeper. The batsman, Mike Smith, had gone down the wicket to do a spot of gardening and he was somewhat surprised to be given out by umpire Kidson. But he was recalled after an outburst of sportsmanship from skipper Goddard who asked for the appeal to be revoked. Poor old Bob Barber broke a finger fielding and couldn't bat in the second innings, but the result was another draw.

England won the rubber with a draw in the fifth Test back at Port Elizabeth. We did have a chance to win the match chasing 246 on the final day but rain intervened again. This was our 13th draw in 15 Tests, which is hardly a run to be proud of but, sometimes, the weather is the one opponent no one can defeat.

I was pleased to finish the tour as England's top wicket-taker with 18, but my happiest memory of the tour featured Kenny Barrington and John Murray. With those two around, laughter was never far behind. Kenny liked to style himself 'the Colonel' and he always called John 'Sergeant Major'. We were in Bulawayo when the Army threw a cocktail party. John politely stepped backwards to let a woman pass and, unfortunately, fell into a fish pond. Barrington, in a loud army voice, shouted, 'Sergeant Major…' and within a few seconds at least half-a-dozen real-life holders of that rank were in attendance. Murray's great boast afterwards was that he had not spilt a drop of his gin and tonic.

But soon it was back to headquarters to start a new phase in my career as the captain of Middlesex. I was very proud to be appointed and I was determined to run things my way. Becoming captain was a huge honour. Alan Moss might have got it; he was not senior to me in experience, but he was older. Being captain didn't increase my salary with Middlesex – there was a maximum wage cap at the club – it just meant I was able to claim a little more in expenses. At that time, we thought we were well paid because we were better paid than footballers, who were themselves subject to the maximum wage.

Although I was captain, I relied heavily for advice and counsel on John Murray and Peter Parfitt. We were firm friends, of course, but it was not just that. We were contemporaries who had been through some of the same battles together and they have very fine cricketing brains. In spite of that, I tried to make it absolutely clear to the rest of the team from the start that I was the man in charge. I remember addressing the players and saying, 'Some of you might think this is a democracy, but some of us here know more than you, so it ain't.' It might not have been exactly Churchillian stuff, but I think the players got the message.

Fortunately for me, the 1965 season started well. I tried to play positive attacking cricket. When it came off, it was wonderful. In our second Championship match of the season, we beat Nottinghamshire at Lord's by five runs with just four minutes to spare after two declarations. Ted Clark hammered a career-best 122 and we rushed to 312 for 6. Don Bennett raced in with 6 wickets and Notts were all out for 188. Then Bob White and I both hit fairly quick scores and we declared again at 174 for 6, setting Notts to make 299 to win in 4 hours and 40 minutes.

I was beginning to worry when they started with an opening stand of 119, but then wickets started falling and I managed to get 4 wickets and Don Bennett mopped up the tail. We had done it in the nick of time and I was in danger of thinking this captaincy lark was a barrel of laughs. Sadly, things did not always go so neatly to plan.

We had a purple patch in June and July and found ourselves at the top of the county Championship. Unfortunately for me, we couldn't maintain that form. Middlesex developed a cricketing version of vertigo and slipped down the table. The bowling was never quite right, with John Price dogged by injury and playing only

12 Championship games. Ron Hooker and myself took our share and Peter Parfitt and Eric Russell scored a lot of runs, but it was never quite enough and, in the end, we finished sixth yet again.

But did get to the semi-final of the Gillette Cup by beating the holders Sussex with some bold attacking cricket that really pleased me. At the time, Sussex were killing the competition with their defensive tactics. If they got in first, they tried to slow down their opponents' scoring rate from the very first ball. I got a lot of satisfaction when we hit 280 against them and had their whole side rattled, especially their captain Ted Dexter. He was so edgy he didn't know what to do for the best. I'd have to be very pressed to have played in any knock-out cup like Ted did.

Middlesex just didn't look at cricket like that; we still had the cavalier spirit of Denis Compton and Bill Edrich running through the club. We were always chatting and joking at the opposition as we played. I'm convinced we enjoyed our cricket more than any other county. Peter Parfitt, John Murray and I were brought up with Denis and Bill who always had a lot to say on the field. That did start a Middlesex revival. But the thing with us was that you never quite knew what we were going to do. We always knew we could beat the best teams in any competition, but there was always a danger that we could lose to the worst. It was great defeating the cup-holders by 90 runs. John Murray hit a 6 and 5 fours in his 49 and Bob Gale struck a sparkling 74 and Peter Parfitt scored 66. That left Sussex needing to score well over four an over, but after some early scares when Ken Suttle and Ted Dexter threatened to break loose, I managed to put the brake on a bit, and Don Bennett broke through with four wickets to give us a place in the last four. I might never have been the most devoted enthusiast for one-day cricket, but there's nothing like reaching the semi-final of the Gillette Cup to perk up your interest. We did score 250 against Surrey in the semi-final, but it was never quite enough and John Edrich (71) and Kenny Barrington (68 not out) saw them home. Still, it was exciting while it lasted.

We had some good players – Mike Selvey came to Middlesex from Surrey when I was captain, and we got on well. He was a very down-to-earth guy with plenty of confidence. You could see early on that the young Mike Gatting was a good player. Once he got in, he could destroy people if he got going, so he was a very handy player to have. He was a strong boy and he could give it a whack.

On the international front, England played New Zealand in a short series of Tests which began in a very chilly Edgbaston in May. It was so cold we had hot drinks brought on twice during the second day, and Kenny Barrington hardly warmed anyone up with a very slow century. He scored 137 in 437 minutes and it resulted in him being dropped for the next Test. I enjoyed bowling against the New Zealanders and took 4 for 18 in their first innings. We won very comfortably by nine wickets.

We won the second Test at Lord's much more narrowly by 7 wickets with just 15 minutes to spare. But the contest turned out to be more memorable at the last Test of the great Freddie Trueman who took his number of victims to 307. It was a record that was to stand for more than ten years until broken by the great West Indian spinner Lance Gibbs. And this was the first Test for John Snow, so it was very much the end of one career and the beginning of another.

The third Test was very one-sided. John Edrich batted for 532 minutes and hit 5 sixes and 52 fours in a marathon innings of 310 not out. In my 21st over, I took the wickets of Yuile, Taylor, Motz and Collinge and, remarkably, that was without completing a hat-trick – the figures showed W0WW0W, and I finished with 5 for 19 in their second innings.

We had a much harder time in the three Tests against the South Africans. We had a chance to win the first Test at Lord's in a contest in which the remarkable fielding of Colin Bland remains one of my strongest memories. I can recall his lightning movements even better than I can remember my 59 not out, so he must have been good. Bland ran out Kenny Barrington and Jim Parks with fantastic throws that hit the stumps. John Edrich had to retire hurt after a ball from Peter Pollock cracked him on the side of the head and, after that, we were always well behind in our race for runs to win.

South Africa won the second Test at Trent Bridge and it

was England's first defeat in 15 matches under Mike Smith's captaincy. The Pollock brothers showed what a formidable double-act they were with Graeme scoring 184 runs and Peter taking 10 for 87 in 48 overs. The visitors ran out victors by 94 runs.

The third Test at The Oval saw us beaten by the weather. We needed 91 to win with 70 minutes left when heavy rain arrived to make sure we could not square the series. After being out of the England side for two years, it was good to see Brian Statham brought back. He took 7 wickets to take his tally to 252, a figure at that time only beaten by his old bowling partner Freddie Trueman. Sadly, that was Brian's swan-song and he was never to play for England again.

9

TOP SPINNING

In the winter of 1965/66, I was delighted to be selected for Mike Smith's team to tour Australia. Just in case any of us were starting to get a little too big-headed, the team flew all the way to Australia in cramped economy class.

I had just about got the feeling back in my legs by the time the Test series opened in Brisbane a few weeks later. Rain interrupted the first day and washed out the second completely, so a positive result was never on the cards. The Aussie batting looked very strong as they scored steadily and declared at 443 for 6 wickets. We thought we had a good shout for Bill Lawry to be out off Brown's seventh ball, but it was not given and he went on to score 166.

Their bowling was pretty sharp as well, and they had us tottering on 86 for 4 at one point. But Kenny Barrington was digging in doggedly and, when I joined him at the crease, I knew we had a chance of avoiding the follow-on. Quite quickly, I found I was seeing the ball really well and I decided that attack was the best policy so, with Kenny still bogged down a little, I started hitting out. Kenny watched my aggressive strokes with growing alarm and then he walked down the pitch and said to me, 'Are you trying to make me look a ★★★★?' He was only half-joking but I almost collapsed with laughter. Kenny was such a great character, you had to laugh. Unfortunately, he was bowled by Neil Hawke soon afterwards and I was left to employ what tactics I chose.

Astonishingly, I put together a score of 60 before Wally Grout stumped me off Philpott and we finished on 280. The Aussies were quick to enforce the follow-on, which they took as a great moral victory, but there was not enough time left for anything other than a draw.

The New Year started pretty violently for me in the second Test at Melbourne. I was unhappy to be demoted to number nine in the order and determined to put my protest in with a decent performance with the bat. It was going well until I caught a ball from Alan Connolly on the back of the head. It knocked me down but, fortunately, I have a hard head and I was soon up. I knew I had to hit back quickly, and I managed three swift boundaries. I was just thinking perhaps I should get hit on the head more often, when the last man was out and I was left on 56 not out. We had scored a massive 558, but the crowd were booing as the game petered out into a draw.

Then, in the third Test at Sydney, we finally got the start we wanted. Batting first, Geoff Boycott and Bob Barber carved out a tremendous opening partnership of 234 in 240 minutes. Boycott was out for 84 but Bob was magnificent that day. He batted for 291 minutes and faced 272 balls in scoring 185 runs. It was his only Test century but it included 19 fours and it was his highest score in first-class cricket and it sent us on the road to victory.

John Edrich picked up where Boycott left off and we had more than 300 runs before the second wicket went down. We reached 488 and then bowled them out for 221 with Brown taking five for 63. This time, it was our turn to enforce the follow-on and it felt great. I scored my 1,000th run in Test cricket in my 14 and, in the second innings, I took 4 for 40 which completed my double in international cricket and helped us to victory by an innings and 93 runs. You don't get victories as emphatic as that over Australia very often and it was highly satisfactory. My fellow spinner David Allen also took four wickets in the second innings and I was really pleased for him. Just because you're rivals doesn't mean that you can't be friends as well.

I was on a bit of a high after that and I could hardly come down to earth in the next match. Centuries came very rarely to me, so I tend to remember the occasions when I reached the magic 100 figure fairly clearly. I certainly recall the match against Northern Country Districts as Mike Smith and I joined forces in a stand of 260 for the sixth wicket.

It was a hot Saturday afternoon in Newcastle and we were chasing the home side's impressive total of 334 and we had not had a good start. We had slipped to 106 for 5 wickets when I joined the captain in the middle. I had a desperately slow start and it took me a quarter-of-an-hour to score my first run. But then Mike got going and I decided to go on the attack as well. He scored 154 and I managed 114 in a highly satisfying case of taking runs to Newcastle.

Australia were definitely still smarting after their defeat at Sydney when the teams met at Adelaide over the New Year holiday for the fourth Test. We were bowled out for 241 with Bob Barber following his heroics with a hapless duck. Simpson and Lawry showed they meant business when they passed our total for the first wicket and they finished on 516. Then Neil Hawke set about our batting with a vengeance. Only Kenny Barrington came off from the frontline batsmen with a typically well-grafted 102. I continued my good form with the bat to register 53 but, in the end, we could not do enough to make Australia bat again and they won by an innings and nine runs.

Kenny Barrington led the way again in the fifth Test at Melbourne as we reached 485 for 9 declared. Kenny hit yet another century and he reached the magic mark with a six, but Bob Cowper struck 307 runs in an extraordinary display of skill and concentration and Australia reached 543 for 8 wickets before declaring. After all those runs, a draw was the only possible result and, although McKenzie took three wickets, we were never in any real danger of losing this match.

Kenny Barrington was the real success of this Australian tour and he topped the batting averages. I was delighted to finish second and ready to head home to a new season in charge of Middlesex by the end of the New Zealand leg, where I finished up largely as a spectator, something that has never come that easily to me.

Middlesex only lost five matches in 1966, which was the same as Yorkshire, who finished the season as champions. Unfortunately, we only won six matches so, under my leadership, the county slipped down to a disappointing 12th-equal in the table. It was, in many ways, a frustrating season. My own form dipped with both ball and bat and so did that of other important team members. Our main, rather fundamental, problem was an inability to bowl out the opposition. John Price bowled pretty well and so did Wes Stewart, a West Indian fast-medium merchant, but Ron Hooker and myself were less effective and, much too often, we drew games we should have won.

But the season was hardly without incident. My friend John Murray scored not one but two centuries against the touring West Indies, for England and for the MCC. And on the personal front, I completed my first hat-trick. It came against Somerset at Weston-super-Mare, admittedly on a far from perfect pitch. Ron Hooker scored a brilliant century in difficult conditions and we won the match by 164 runs. Ron rattled up a six and 13 fours in his 102 which took just 89 minutes. The rest of the batting collapsed and we were all out for 239.

Somerset replied with 158, thanks mainly to a hard-hitting 55 from Langford. In turn, we were skittled out in our second innings for just 126, which left Somerset to score a far-from-impossible 208 for victory. But John Price took 6 wickets for 12 runs and I took my hat-trick and they were all out for 43. It was an extraordinary match.

The Single Wicket Champion of England was an imposing title and I was delighted to accept it in mid-August after a fairly hectic competition at Lord's that had the added bonus of deeply irritating one Geoffrey Boycott, that well-known Yorkshireman. It was a tense contest with some high-quality opposition. I managed to beat Keith Stackpole of Australia in the first round thanks to a spectacular direct hit run-out from a young fielder and then came up against Boycott in the semi-final. I scored 56 not out off my eight overs and even managed a six. Boycott was doing quite well until he spooned a catch to forward short-leg. He was typically ungracious in defeat, complaining bitterly that the Lord's ground staff had fielded much more enthusiastically for my bowling than for his. He swore blind afterwards that the boys tried a lot harder for me than they did for him. 'They're all on your side because you're the local boy,' he moaned.

I just said, 'Don't be so bloody silly.'

Dear old Geoffrey. No one could ever accuse him of being a good loser. Geoffrey could bowl quite well; he wasn't a mug. Even on tour, he was a loner. He never did have many friends. In the final, I met Bob Cowper, the Australian Test player, and won relatively easily thanks to a sharp stumping from my pal John Murray. It was a great day, even if it was exhausting, and the first prize of £250 was very useful.

Geoffrey Boycott's awkwardness sometimes worked against him. We faced him in an end-of-season match at the Scarborough Festival where he needed 12 to get his century and Yorkshire needed 18 to win the match. So we said, 'Sod you, Geoffrey,' because he had already kept us there an awful long while, so we tossed them up to Don Wilson at the other end and he hit three fours to win the match. Everybody plays their shots in these games, apart from Geoffrey Boycott, of course. It didn't matter, but we thought we'd leave him high and dry on 88 not out, rather than let him bore his way to another tedious 100. He was a good player, but he had a difficult personality. It's a team game, after all, and he wasn't much of a laugh.

England got off to a bad start in the Test series against the West Indies. Conrad Hunte square cut the very first ball at Old Trafford for four runs and the visitors hardly looked back. Hunte hit 135 and Sobers an elegant 161. I thought I had bowled reasonably well for my 5 for 85, but there was no doubt as to who was on top, particularly after Lance Gibbs had spun us out for 167. Following on was no fun either as, in spite of a spirited 94 from that great character Colin Milburn on his Test début, we were bowled out for 277 and lost the match by an innings and 40 runs.

Colin became a good friend and I was often an enthusiastic member of an audience fortunate enough to hear him singing. Everyone remembers his somewhat spherical figure, which never looked as if it had been designed with competitive sport in mind, but I like to think of his wonderful voice which has lit up many an enjoyable evening. But even he at his ebullient best with the bat could not prevent defeat and we lost inside three days for the first time since before the war.

The second Test at Lord's was much more closely contested. Some fine bowling from Ken Higgs restricted Gary Sobers and his men to 269 and, with Tom Graveney and Jim Parks both hitting 90s, we finished on 355 with a decent lead. We made a good start on their second innings as they slumped to 95 for 5, before Gary Sobers and his cousin David Holford came together to stop the rot with a partnership of 274. It was record-breaking as well as heart-breaking. It was the highest sixth-wicket knock in West Indies Test history and it ruthlessly removed our chance of victory and squaring the series. England needed to score 284 runs in 240 minutes to win and the way Colin Milburn set off it looked as if it might even be possible. He hit a sparkling 126 not out but the support was not there and we ran out of time.

At Nottingham, a young spinner called Derek Underwood made his début and Ray Illingworth returned to the Test team as I found myself dropped from the line-up for the third Test at Trent Bridge. My form had not been good and I could not argue with the decision. Ray and I never really minded being replaced by each other too much, but no one likes being dropped. But I'd hardly be human if I hadn't granted myself at least a wry smile when West Indies won the match by 139 runs and Derek and Ray didn't manage a wicket between them.

Mind you, I was brought back into the fold for the fourth Test at Headingley and we lost that by an innings and 55 runs. Gary Sobers scored 174 to lead his side to 500 for 9 declared and then proceeded to take 8 England wickets. Sobers was a phenomenal player; he struck 103 runs between lunch and tea on the second day.

With the series decided, I found myself excluded again for the consolation victory England achieved at The Oval. We bowled them out for 268 and then scored a remarkable 527. Tom Graveney ran up 165 but then wickets fell fast until an extraordinary late revival, sparked by my old friend John Murray. He went in at number nine and then proceeded to show everyone what a fine batsman he could be with a stylish knock of 112 before Gary Sobers had him leg before wicket. With bowlers Higgs and Snow giving the batsmen a lesson with 63 and 59 respectively, this was a brilliant climax to the innings. Even better was bowling the West Indies out for 225 to win by an innings and 34 runs.

Worcester was always one of my favourite grounds. It

seemed to suit my style of play and I always enjoyed myself even more if I managed to wind up my old pal and rival spinner Norman Gifford. Norman had a notoriously short fuse on the pitch, although, afterwards, he was as easy-going as you like. But I got him one day by constantly backing away from the stumps as he was about to bowl at me. I complained about spectators moving behind Norman's arm, about paper bags blowing around in my line of vision, anything to knock Norman out of his rhythm. Eventually, a plane flew over from Heathrow and Norman stopped halfway through his run up and said, 'What about the plane, Fred? Shall I wait until the pilot sits down?'

My old form seemed to be returning in 1967 as I did the 'double' for the first time since 1962, but I found it hard to lift Middlesex. We finished a dull seventh in the County Championship and the season was largely excitement-free for a number of reasons, apart from an epic tied match against Hampshire at Portsmouth.

On the Test front, I was not selected for the series against India, which meant I was fortunate enough not to have to watch Geoffrey Boycott's famously slow 246 not out which led to his being dropped for disciplinary reasons. His first 100 took a monumental 341 minutes and, even for a Yorkshireman, this was seriously boring cricket. England won the Test by six wickets and also took the second Test when the action moved to headquarters and I was happy to see John Murray take six catches in the first innings to equal a Test record. England completed a hat-trick in the three-match series with a comfortable victory at Edgbaston.

Pakistan were also touring England that summer, with the series beginning at Lord's with Robin Hobbs and Ray Illingworth in charge of the spin bowling. John Murray managed a 'pair' by not scoring in either innings, and I tried hard not to remind him of this disaster more often than twice a day.

I was brought back into the side for the second Test at Trent Bridge where we swept to a convincing ten-wicket victory. It was a low-scoring match in which the most impressive performance came from the Nottingham Fire Brigade who pumped away 100,000 gallons of water from the ground after a violent thunderstorm just after tea on the first day. We bowled the tourists out for 140 and then scored 252 for 8 wickets declared. Then Pakistan were bowled out again for 114, thanks, mainly, to a five-wicket haul by Derek Underwood, although I did bag a couple, including the wicket of the talented Asif Iqbal. He was caught at long-on by a young recruit to the Nottinghamshire playing staff called Alan Bull, who was fielding as substitute for Basil D'Oliveira. Strangely, he was destined never to play in a full first-class match.

At any rate, I kept my place for the third Test at The Oval. I grabbed a couple of wickets as we bowled them out for 216 and then Kenny Barrington hammered his third century in successive Tests. It was the first time he had hit 100 in a Test on his home ground and he was delighted. For the record books, he also became the first England player to hit hundreds on the six current Test grounds. But he told me later he was just happy to have played well. He was bang on top of his game and helped encourage me to have a good knock. I finished on 65 as we reached 440 by the end of the innings. After that, Pakistan were very much on the back foot and Ken Higgs took five wickets as we had a comfortable win by eight wickets.

You could say England's winter tour to the West Indies was fairly memorable. It included a Test match where the official result was 'riot stopped play', and my part in the trip ended when I had four toes chopped off by the propeller of a motorboat.

Yet it had all started hopefully enough. I was delighted to be chosen as vice-captain of the side, which was to be skippered by Colin Cowdrey. Having been captain of the side that had been comprehensively beaten by the West Indies in 1966, Colin was determined to make a success of the job. He turned to me and two other senior pros, Kenny Barrington and Jim Parks, to help organise some intensive training before we flew off on 27 December 1967.

Colin was not a great captain but he always meant well. He announced, 'There is no time for a leisurely approach, you cannot just drift into a tour, and I will see that we are a team before we leave England. We seek maximum fitness and to be mentally conditioned for the type of cricket played out there. We have 16 very experienced players who can end a very lean spell for England.' Colin struck his positive note and Kenny and I posed for suitably determined-looking publicity photographs.

In the first Test at Port of Spain, Trinidad, it all started very well. Kenny and Tom Graveney both got centuries in the first innings and we built an impressive total of 568. In spite of an attractive 118 from a young batsman called Clive Lloyd, the West Indies could manage only 363 and we enforced the follow-on. It looked as if a famous victory was possible when Brown took three second innings wickets in the last over before tea. But Wes Hall partnered Sobers throughout the final session and we were forced to settle for a draw.

The second Test in Kingston, Jamaica, looked like following a similar line as we scored 376, including 101 from captain Cowdrey, and then we got into their batting. John Snow bowled Sobers first ball and took six other wickets as the West Indies were bowled out for 143. Everything was going well as we got stuck into their second innings on the fourth day and Jim Parks caught Basil Butcher off Basil D'Oliveira. Basil knew he was out and he walked even before umpire Douglas Sang-Hue could give a decision.

All of a sudden, all hell was let loose and bottles started flying on to the pitch and the police over-reacted by spraying tear gas all over the place. It really was 'riot stopped play' and it was pretty frightening for a time.

This was a very tense political time in Jamaica and a lot

of the wild crowd scenes were nothing to do with the cricket. All the same, poor old Colin was hit by a bottle and there was widespread panic for a while as people scrambled to get away from the tear gas. It even blew into the press box, thus ensuring even larger headlines and a sitting of the Jamaican cabinet was suspended.

But when order was restored and play resumed after a delay of 70 minutes, England had lost their impetus. Sobers and David Holford were able to last out the day and then go on to set us 159 to win at a run a minute. It was never really on, but after Gibbs and Sobers had grabbed three wickets, we found ourselves clinging on for the draw on 68 for 8 at the end.

We flew off to Barbados in preparation for the third Test and, just as I least expected it, disaster struck. A large group of players and journalists were on the beach and swimming in the sea near the Sandy Lane Hotel. I was in the water with a few others and we swam up to a motorboat. We were all round the boat, floating around out of our depth, so we just held on to the side of the boat and chatted, our legs floating flat out on the surface. I didn't know that this boat had a peculiar design – the propeller was placed in the middle of the hull, instead of at the back. My feet bobbed up and suddenly there was a bang. We'd been in the water some time so I thought my feet were a bit numb. I said, 'Hold on a minute, I think I've cut my foot,' so I raised my left leg out of the water… and, oh my God, it looked quite a mess.

We wrapped a towel round my bleeding foot and then I was carried to a car by Denis Compton, of all people, who was out there covering the tour as a journalist, and Brian Johnston, the BBC commentator. At that point in my life, I certainly needed people to keep my spirits up and it's hard to think of anyone better equipped that those two. We were about to rush off to Bridgetown, when a young boy who had witnessed what had happened told us to go the opposite way where there was a small hospital with a 'famous doctor'.

The lad was right. There was a hospital very nearby run by the nuns, and there was a Canadian surgeon, Dr Homer C Rogers, who used to come down to work in Barbados. Fortunately for me, he had a great deal of experience working with ice hockey injuries, so my severed toes was nothing new to him. When he examined my foot, I could only bear to look at him, not the injury. He said, 'Oh we'll soon have that sorted out,' in such a bright, confident way that I started to relax a little. He said he had seen dozens of ice hockey players get back into the game after having toes sliced off. He gave me fantastic confidence when I thought my career was all but over.

Amazingly, it never really hurt that badly. Two of the toes were sliced straight off and two others were just hanging on with a sliver of skin. The surgeon wrapped the skin over my foot and I was left with just my big toe. All this was to prevent problems with arthritis and the fact that I lived in England with its cold winters. I must say that, to this day, I've never really had a problem with my foot at all.

When I first went into the hospital, there was a little old lady sitting in a chair who asked me if I was the young man who had lost some toes. 'What a shame,' she said, 'what a pity.' But when I looked more closely at her, I realised she had no legs. So there was no chance of my feeling too sorry for myself.

Dr Rogers was confident from the start that I would be able to play again. He reassured me that he had done many similar operations in his career and, in every case, the patients were walking without discomfort or handicap within a few weeks. He said I was 'lucky' because the propeller had only grazed my big toe. If it had been chopped off, my balance would have gone for ever, but the ball of my foot was fine so he insisted I would be walking and playing cricket in a matter of weeks, not months. He also told me not to use a walking stick, as that could affect my balance if I began to rely upon it too much. When he heard that I had been dancing – or, more realistically, shuffling – only a few days after the accident, he realised I was definitely on the road to recovery.

It might not have looked too pretty, but I soon found out that I could walk, and run and bowl pretty much as before. I sought some advice from a London ballet school to help train me to restore my balance and, only eight weeks later, I was playing again. I returned to cricket in a match in Münchengladbach, Germany, against a British army team. I flew out to test my injured foot playing for the Cricketers' Club of London. The club was owned and managed by Frank Russell, a great friend of mine who, today, still takes a keen interest in cricket at the age of 91. Obviously, I was nervous but I had trained on it and I knew it felt fine. As it turned out, I got 63 runs and took 6 wickets for 44 runs and my foot held up brilliantly. It never affected me after that at all. At first, I was concerned that it might have an impact on my bowling because my left foot was the one I swivelled on when I bowled. I used to go out with a rubber boot on my left foot so it would turn as I bowled, and a proper studded cricket boot on my right foot. But when I realised it was not hurting, I went back to an ordinary pair of boots. I was mightily relieved that it nothing seemed to have changed, and considered myself very lucky. In fact, I recovered so quickly I was back for that season with Middlesex.

That incident left me wondering why we ever bother to have toes in the first place. The only real problem the accident left me with was counting — afterwards, I always had trouble going over 16!

After some time, I was awarded compensation for my loss. It amounted to £98, which didn't quite measure up to my valuation of the loss. Less than £25 a toe did not seem exactly generous, to say the least. And perhaps the other little known fact from this sad and bizarre incident was that the identity of the driver of the boat was never made public. Penny Cowdrey, the wife of the England captain, was sitting at the wheel of the boat when the accident happened. Although she was completely innocent of any fault, her husband Colin was very concerned that her name was kept out of all of the coverage. After all, 'ENGLAND SKIPPER'S WIFE CHOPS OFF HIS DEPUTY'S TOES' would have been a much better story. But it is an illustration of the good relationship the players then had with the gentlemen of the press that Penny's name was never mentioned. If it had happened today, I don't think the journalists would have been quite so restrained.

I was able to resume my Middlesex career, but it was a different story as far as England was concerned. At the time, I was a regular player and the England vice-captain, but this injury let my old rival Raymond Illingworth in. Although I was playing cricket again very quickly as far as Test matches were concerned, they were not prepared to take a chance on me, so Raymond came in. He captained the side because he was a pretty good captain, so that kicked me out for a couple of years.

I was 35 years old when I had my accident. There are cricketers who call it a day around that age, even if they have a full complement of toes, but I never considered retiring. I loved the game too much, and the prospect of working for a living was definitely not attractive!

My county form was pretty good. It could have been a reaction to all those jokes about putting my best foot forward and so on, but I took 100 wickets in the

Championship and finished top of the batting averages. But the side continued to struggle and I took the decision to step down from the captaincy. I was not getting the best out of the other players and it seemed the only course of action. It was a decision I took with some regret, as I said at the time that I was giving up the best job in cricket – and I meant it.

Cricket was my life but, at that time, I felt as if I was playing with the weight of the world on my shoulders. We had a sequence of games that we failed to win when we should have done and it affected me deeply. We weren't doing that badly, but we had a good enough side to be doing better. I took the captain's job very seriously and it was starting to get to me. As soon as the decision was announced, I knew I had done the right thing. It felt as if an enormous weight had been lifted from my shoulders.

Peter Parfitt took over from me as captain and we instantly won the last four matches but, sadly, the improvement did not last for long into the next season. Peter was hardly helped when his appointment was not confirmed for quite a while, but I was too busy struggling with my own poor form to be a great deal of help. And if 1969 was a poor season, then 1970 was to be even worse as Middlesex finished second from bottom, our worst result since 1930. But on the bright side, to confirm that my foot injury had not affected my cricket, I bowled more than 1,000 overs in the season and was one of only four spinners to take over 100 wickets. The match I enjoyed the most was a Gillette Cup first-round tie against Norfolk which brought Bill Edrich back to Lord's at the age of 54. We won by 147 runs but Bill smacked a lively 36 and ended his innings with 22 from just 6 balls.

In 1971, Mike Brearley took over the captaincy. Like many people, I felt Peter Parfitt was a much better cricketer, but Mike was full of motivational theories and he became the new broom who was going to sweep in a new era at Lord's. I was enjoying my cricket and I took 100 wickets for the 16th season in my career, and I enjoyed bowling in tandem with a spinner called Phillippe Edmonds, like Brearley, another young, ex-university man with a big future in the game.

Peter Parfitt retired at the end of 1972, which I felt was a great pity. He was still good enough to play for England in the last three Tests against Australia that season but, sadly, I think he had had enough of Middlesex. Another old friend and fine batsman, Eric Russell, also left, but I bowled and batted on through the changing times.

10

TOTAL RECALL

After the accident and then the end of my marriage, I did find myself very hard up. I met a lovely girl called Stephanie Hughan and we were very short of cash. That was really the big reason I kept playing; I was not qualified to do anything else.

In September 1973, I married Stephanie, a Yorkshire girl, no less, and we have thoroughly enjoyed my last few years playing cricket, being a selector, running a post office and shop and, more recently, retirement. Much of our time nowadays is spent on Mallorca, where we love having old cricketing friends out to stay.

But back in 1973 there were still records to beat and I enjoyed an excellent August during which I took 30 of my season's haul of 72. This total took me past JT Hearne's record aggregate of 2,093 wickets for Middlesex. An eager statistician rushed to inform me that I had become just the fourth player in history – behind WG Grace, George Hirst and Wilfred Rhodes – to reach 20,000 runs and 2,500 wickets in first-class cricket. Now if accolades like that don't make a bloke feel old, then I don't know what does!

I was enjoying my cricket as much as ever. John Murray scored his first century for Middlesex since 1969 and then went on and scored another in the next match, just to show that the old guard had a contribution to make. I took seven wickets in each innings of the match against Yorkshire to help Middlesex to a comfortable eight-wicket win.

Geoffrey Boycott could never be accused of being one of the world's great humourists, but he did make me smile when we played Yorkshire at Middlesbrough. Mike Brearley had not been captain for long, but he had already developed an irritating habit of trying to set my field for me when I was bowling. I never minded advice, so long as it coincided closely with my own views, but I thought that Mike had some daft ideas. I was bowling to Geoff Boycott and Brearley insisted on fielding at forward short-leg. It inhibited the way I wanted to bowl, so I asked him to move... and he wouldn't. Boycott duly crashed the ball and almost hit Brearley. Brearley complained that Boycott tried to hit him. Boycott observed that if he had wanted to hit him, he would have done. I found it hard to sympathise too much with our captain.

The 'partnership' between myself and Phil Edmonds

certainly prospered and, in 1974, we took 156 wickets between us while the rest of the Middlesex bowlers managed just 116. The Honourable Timothy Lamb, an Oxford Blue no less, bowled 94 overs and took 5 wickets for 270 runs. To be fair, Tim was a nice chap who became a friend. Years later, he was to become Chief Executive of the ECB. He was quite a useful bowler, but he suffered a little with his accuracy. I tried to encourage him and said, 'Come on, Tim. You have to practice, practice, practice.' That's something I have always believed in, particularly when things were not going well. Tim replied that it was not for him. In a rash moment, I told him that perhaps that was why he was the 'peehole bowler he was'.

Years before, I remember having a discussion with Ron Hooker about his bowling and trying to help him with his line and length. I told him he should bowl 'there and not there'. He replied, 'It's all right for you, Fred. You're an England player. If I could do that, I would be playing for England, too.'

That made me realise that there's no point in false modesty. I could bowl better and bat better than some people, so I had to be more realistic about what I demanded. Ron was doing the best he could and that is all you can demand of anyone. If someone bowls a bad ball and gives away some needless runs, there is no point in going up and saying, 'What on earth do you think you are doing?' They know they have made a mistake and they are already doing their best. But until Ron Hooker said that,

I had this instinctive feeling that all professional cricketers were roughly the same standard and all were capable of excellence. Unfortunately, that is simply not true. It changed my attitude to other players.

At the time, I wasn't playing for England, of course, but then, miraculously, I was back in the fold. The recall to the national side came in August 1974 when I was less than three months away from my 42nd birthday. I had been out of the England team for the six years since my accident in Barbados, and I thought my chance had gone. I was all fixed up to go to South Africa to do more coaching for the winter, but some members of the press had rooted for me and I think that helped.

I should add that I was absolutely overjoyed. I knew I was just as good a player after the accident as I was before but, while Ray Illingworth was captain, he was hardly likely to drop himself and install me. I had never entirely given up hope of a recall; I just never thought I would have had to wait that long. Playing for your country is the ultimate ambition of any player and, even after you have played 49 times, the desire to be selected does not go away.

Alec Bedser was the chairman of the selectors and I think he had always rated me. I had been playing pretty well, so I knew I was in with a chance. The news was announced in a typically English cricketing fashion over the Tannoy at Lord's just as I was bowling at Jack Birkenshaw. I felt a little sorry for Jack as he had four times been 12th man for England that summer, and he was hearing that he had been left behind. Then, two balls later I had him caught at backward short-leg.

The messages of congratulation and support that I received warmed my heart. I believed I could be our best slow bowler on a good pitch and, clearly, the selectors felt the same way. Chairman of the selectors Alec Bedser, who was to manage the tour, said significantly, 'Our cupboard is pretty bare when it comes to young players. We spent four-and-a-half hours picking this party and, although Titmus's age and lack of toes have always been a factor against him, we decided that proven ability mattered most.'

Of course, there were the usual questions about my fitness but that had never been a problem. I knew I could bowl all day if necessary, but I was not as fast in the field as I used to be. I knew they would just have to be a little choosey about where they asked me to field. Mike Denness was to captain the side and John Edrich was vice-captain.

Geoffrey Boycott was brought back after being dropped that summer and the rest of the party was Dennis Amiss, Geoff Arnold, Keith Fletcher, Tony Greig, Mike Hendrick, Alan Knott, Peter Lever, David Lloyd, Chris Old, Bob Taylor, Derek Underwood and Bob Willis.

The press who had campaigned to get me in the party were quick to point out that Mike Hendrick and Bob Willis were both babies when my first-class cricketing career had started in 1949. I didn't mind that, I was just thrilled to be given another chance at an age when most players have retired. I said at the time, 'I will be the new old boy in the party,' and I meant it.

Before we left for Australia, Middlesex finished sixth in the County Championship and I think I was still pinching myself when we flew off. It was my first tour, indeed my first MCC game, for nearly seven years. Geoffrey Boycott had pulled out of the tour to be replaced by Brian Luckhurst. Geoffrey was still locked into his self-imposed exile from Test cricket. As we flew out, he said he wouldn't be thinking about us because he was working so hard on his benefit. What a charmer. But as my thoughts switched to the surprise challenge of another Test series, I realised I was not nearly as nervous or tense as when previous tours approached. I knew I could not make or break my career in Australia because I was already at the back end of it, so my mental state was noticably different from that of other players. Obviously, my aim was to give of my best but, while no one could know how they would feel when the crunch came, I felt I would be more relaxed than before. There had to be some sort of bonus for all that age and experience, and freedom from tension is essential for a spin bowler. I knew I was as fit as I could be at my age, and I knew I was bowling well.

I was pleased that my wife Stephanie and our daughter Tandy, along with Stephanie's parents, were able to come out to Australia. But the authorities stipulated rather embarrassingly that wives were only to spend three weeks sleeping in the players' hotel. There were lots of jokes about whether 21 nights were quite enough to sustain normal appetites over a tour of five months. Or whether, indeed, 21 nights might be too much for some couples who were no longer close. I'll only say that I'm glad there was no one monitoring how many nights this player sneaked off to spend the night in his wife's hotel. It was an international cricket tour, not a holiday, so I suppose the powers-that-be were just trying to do the right thing. I did feel, though, that at my age nobody should be telling me whether to sleep with my wife or not!

I often shared a room on tour with Derek Underwood. I think, perhaps, there is an affinity between spinners as the job definitely has different demands from almost everything else that happens on the cricket field. Players are great mickey-takers and Derek and I soon acquired new nicknames. Presumably, because of the difference in our ages and my accident, some wag called us 'Steptoe and Son' and it stuck! Derek is a great cricketer and a likeable fellow and I really enjoyed his company.

Flying to Australia was a great deal quicker than going by boat, and I was grateful for that. I was also grateful that conversations about my recall to the England camp after a six-year break and aged 41 were starting to die down. I only ever wanted to be one of the team. Henry Blofeld kindly recorded that I had been a good influence on the strong team spirit that was developing among the party. Henry said, 'Wherever he is, a smile is always on his lips,' but I was hoping to be more than team comedian.

Poor Mike Denness, the skipper, was certainly not laughing much. He was laid low with a heavy cold just when he wanted to be at his perkiest. I was pleased when the cricket started and I grabbed three wickets in the match against a Victoria Country XI. We flew up to Port Lincoln and our visit coincided with another great sporting event. After an excellent lunch of enormous prawns in a local hotel, we all crowded into a small upper room to watch Muhammad Ali fight George Foreman. What a battle! Meanwhile, the captain's condition worsened and he was taken to hospital with Alec Bedser blaming 'abdominal trouble'. Denness had been ill since we had arrived Down Under and, although he played in the opening first class match against South Australia, he was clearly in some discomfort. I felt very sorry for Mike because he had done a good job of getting everyone else into a positive frame of mind. But after undergoing comprehensive tests in hospital in Melbourne, he was finally pronounced fit and well.

Back in England, the newspapers were full of the disappearance of Lord Lucan. We were blissfully unaware of most day-to-day news, just delighted to be reunited with our captain. Mike was well enough to play in a morale-boosting win over New South Wales, but my own morale was less boosted as I was not in the team.

But as we headed towards Queensland and the first Test in Brisbane, I was in the 13 selected for the match against the strong state side. I had only played one first-class match so far, and I desperately needed a chance to show what I could do. Also, as I may have said more than once before, I much prefer playing cricket to watching it. But I was left out of the side against Queensland so I had to watch from the sidelines to get a glimpse of Australia's exciting fast bowler Jeff Thomson. He was only 21 then and that day he lacked control, but you could see the potential and also get a taste of the impressive speed. In the second innings, he rattled Keith Fletcher on the elbow.

As the first Test approached, it was clear Derek Underwood was going to get in the side and I was not. I tried to keep my disappointment to myself and be positive towards my room-mate and friend. Australia won the toss and batted and a determined stand between Ian Chappell and his brother Greg took the score slowly over 200. Bob Willis was our most successful bowler with 3 for 29. Derek took two late wickets which cheered England a little, and the day finished with the home side on 219 for 6 wickets.

The next day, the Australians were bowled out for 309 and the match seemed poised fairly evenly. But then came the onslaught from Lillee and Thomson. Bowling with astonishing ferocity, Thomson had both of our openers out as we reached double figures. Dennis Amiss and Brian Luckhurst were both rushed into unwise shots and caught. John Edrich dug into his reserves of bravery and experience and stuck around somehow. But Mike Denness was lbw to Walker for 6 and Keith Fletcher was bowled by Lillee for 17. England were 57 for 4 and the Australians were threatening to bowl England out for less than the 110 that was needed to avoid the follow-on.

Then Tony Greig decided attack was possibly the best form of defence. Not since Ted Dexter took on Charlie Griffith and Wesley Hall in the memorable 1963 Test against the West Indies at Lord's had I seen anything quite like it. Greig played and missed quite a few times, but he rode his luck and took the match right back to the home side. Greig ducked under the bouncers and then drew himself up to his full height and made as if to head the ball to the boundary, which drew glowers of disapproval from both Lillee and Thomson. But he stuck around and scored an invaluable 110, which helped England ease to 265, only 44 runs behind, which seemed impossible at one stage.

Australia replied by scoring 288 runs for the loss of 5 wickets and then declaring to try to dislodge the England openers before the light faded. They did not succeed in that but, on the last day, Jeff Thomson took 6 for 46 to bowl England out for a sorry 166 and win the match. My pal Derek Underwood was top scorer with 30 as all of our batsmen failed.

The mood in the camp was pretty sombre after that trouncing. And we were forced to send out a call for reinforcements. We had already lost David Lloyd to a broken finger in practice, and it seemed John Edrich was suffering a recurrence of his old back trouble. A message went back to London to call up Colin Cowdrey to fly out. I was happy with the decision; after all, Colin was almost as old as me!

Just when England thought their injury crisis could not get any worse, it did. An X-ray revealed that Dennis Amiss had suffered a broken thumb off a ball from Jeff Thomson and would therefore miss the second Test in Perth. We flew across to the other side of Australia in some five-and-a-half hours and I was pleased to find myself in the team to play Western Australia. It was a match again dominated from an English point of view by Tony Greig. He struck an imperious 167 and Alan Knott fired 62, but the match was lost by 120 runs in the end. The only plus point for me was that I had a good bowl, in tandem with Greig, and had a lot of what I thought were confident lbw appeals turned down. But I was delighted to be selected for the Second Test.

With Edrich and Amiss injured, Colin Cowdrey was forced straight into action in the Test, just four days after he had arrived in Australia. Ian Chappell won the toss and then sent England in to face his formidable pace duo. At first, it seemed we were going to make a real game of it as David Lloyd crafted 49 runs and helped ease us to 99 runs for the loss of only one wicket. Unfortunately, Lloyd was then out and, in the next 11 overs, 4 more wickets fell for the addition of only 33 runs. England were 132 for 6 shortly after tea and, soon afterwards, all out for 208. Alan Knott and myself did manage to put together a stand of 62 for the seventh wicket, but it was not nearly enough. The date of Friday 13th seemed significant as we looked back over a sequence of disasters that made up our innings.

The Australian batsmen were brimful of confidence as we struggled to keep them within reach of our meagre first-innings score. I did take a couple of wickets but centuries from Edwards and Walters helped them to a total of 481 and we knew the writing was on the wall.

In our second innings, poor Brian Luckhurst had a hand too bruised to allow him to open the innings and Colin Cowdrey volunteered to take his place. Considering he had only just arrived, this was brave and, for a while, it seemed as if it might even pay off. He was dropped before scoring but then went on to build up an innings of 41 before Thomson trapped him lbw. Colin played so many fine shots it showed that it was possible to bat against the Aussie attack. Poor David Lloyd took a very fast ball from Thomson in the pit of his stomach and had to retire hurt, though he came back later in the innings.

At the end of the third day, we were 102 for the loss of Cowdrey's wicket and it seemed as if Denness and Greig might be at the start of a decent stand. Unfortunately, it did not turn out like that. Before the scheduled end of the fourth day, we were all out for 293 and 2 down in the series. Grieg square-cut the first ball of the day for four, but then mis-timed a drive and was caught in the slips. Denness was caught to an awful shot soon afterwards, and Fletcher was caught behind soon after that. We were 124 for 4 and all hope of avoiding defeat was realistically long gone.

At that stage, Thomson had taken 3 wickets for 4 runs in 15 balls. Alan Knott and David Lloyd, who had boldly returned to the fray, were out soon afterwards and I found myself in the middle with Brian Luckhurst. I concentrated hard and tried to get right behind the line and even began to deal with the pace. Brian went and Chris Old came in and we had a stand that at least took us past the Australian first innings. But then Chris was out and I thought I had better go on the attack before I ran out of partners. I heaved at one from Mallett and Greg Chappell caught me out for 61, which, sadly, was our top score. Strangely, Greg's catch gave him seven for the match which beat a record that was so old it was held by his grandfather. But obscure statistics are no comfort when you're two matches down against the Australians with a frightening injury list and a skipper sadly out of form.

I was very pleased for Mike Denness when he found a bit of form at last in the match against South Australia. He hit 88 not out and looked in pretty good shape. And with Dennis Amiss and John Edrich returned to fitness, the side had a much better look about it as we took the field at Melbourne on Boxing Day, determined not to lose three Tests on the trot. We batted first and made a pretty moderate 242 as only Alan Knott with 52 and John Edrich with 49 really performed. Jeff Thomson bowled very fast again and deserved his figures of 4 for 72.

It looked ominous when Australia went in to bat and moved to 65 without loss. Mike Hendrick pulled a hamstring muscle in only his third over and was out of the rest of the match, so our attack was instantly in trouble. But Bob Willis redoubled his efforts and bowled really well to take 5 for 61 and Tony Greig and I each managed to get a couple of wickets and we restricted the home side to 241. It was only a single run, but never before had a first-innings lead felt better.

I couldn't persuade the umpires to give out lbw any batsmen who missed the ball while sweeping, otherwise my figures would have been better. But Alan Knott did well to take a fine catch when Rodney Marsh mistimed a sweep and gloved the ball towards short-leg. Alan was very quick and I was grateful, because that was my 150th Test wicket.

In our second innings, Dennis Amiss hit a fine 90 to give us a real chance of taking a grip on the match but only Tony Greig, who scored 60, and David Lloyd with 48, provided any sort of support. Everyone else, apart from Bob Willis on 15, was in single figures, which was pretty dreadful. I got a duck, so I was in no position to criticise. Unfortunately, I stayed around long enough to get a painful whack on the knee from a very quick ball from Jeff Thomson. Amiss played so well that Dennis Lillee lost his cool and the umpires had to tell him, via skipper Ian Chappell, to calm down.

On a lighter note, Tony Greig waltzed into the dressing room one morning with Shirley Bassey in tow. Alec Bedser was shocked. He took a quick look and demanded to know what on earth Greigy thought he was doing bringing a woman into our all-male sanctuary. I quickly tried to explain to an outraged Alec that it was not just any woman but the great Shirley Bassey, and that most of the lads would be thrilled to meet her. I have to say, she has always been one of my favourite singers. Alec mumbled something unrepeatable and shuffled off.

As the final day opened, Australia were 4 for no wicket needing 246 runs to win. By the end, Australia were 238 for 8 wickets and, although the match was a draw, both sides had come very close to victory. Greg Chappell hit a very determined 61 and I was delighted to get him lbw. My knee hurt a bit but it held up pretty well for me to bowl 29 overs and take 2 for 64. I would have had another wicket, but Mike Denness dropped a fairly easy catch at mid-on off Redpath. It was unlike the captain, who was normally a very good fielder, but I'm afraid the pressure was getting to him. After a string of disappointing innings, there was a growing argument for him to drop himself for the fourth Test. But before then, there was widespread relief among our party that at least we had made a game of the third match. Perhaps the Australians were not really as wonderful as we thought they were.

On New Year's Eve, we even won a one-day international against Australia, though I think for both sides this was really something of a non-event. We all knew the Tests were the serious business of the tour. But Greg Chappell gave an indication of Australian attitudes when he ran out Brian Luckhurst when he was backing up a little too much. Chappell had warned Luckhurst earlier, but it was hardly an action likely to generate goodwill between the teams.

Poor Mike Denness did what all the pundits advised was the decent thing and dropped himself for the fourth Test at Sydney. I was surprised by his action. We have all been through bad patches, but if you believe in your own ability – and, if you don't, you shouldn't be out there – then surely you pick yourself if you have the authority. I don't think I would ever drop myself as captain, but then I'm an optimist who always thinks things are going to turn out all right!

Vice-captain John Edrich took charge and it was a bad-tempered Test match. Tony Greig was warned for bowling too many short balls at Dennis Lillee, which was fairly ridiculous as there was no way Tony could be accused of generating enough speed to intimidate the paceman seriously. After all the English ribs that had been rattled by Lillee and Thomson in the series up to that point, we felt the sudden outburst of Australian anguish was a bit rich, to say the least. But it did, sadly, sour the atmosphere for a while. Lillee threw his bat away and pretended to be in agony after being hit by Greig on the shoulder. We England fielders could hardly restrain ourselves and Keith Fletcher in the gully laughed out loud. Keith handed Lillee his bat back and asked him how it felt to be hit. 'If you stand there for a second, you'll find out,' said the angry Australian.

We looked as if we were going to restrict the home side to a reasonable start until their tail-enders began blasting some late runs. Derek Underwood and myself, or 'Steptoe and Son' to our team-mates, were ready and waiting to try to curb this late onslaught, but we were not called upon. It was a great pity because, I thought we worked well together. It worked for me because often the batsmen found they could not hit Derek and became frustrated and tried to hit me, and it is when they are trying to hit you that they are most vulnerable.

Australia finished on 405 and, by the end of the day, we had lost three valuable wickets for just 106. Already, a draw look about all we could aim for. Thanks largely to a brave 82 from Alan Knott, we managed to get to 295. I almost got going with Alan and I really enjoyed myself, hitting 22 before I tried one cut too many and was caught behind.

Dennis Lillee remained at the foot of all English popularity polls by bowling a vicious beamer at Bob Willis. Australia made 289 for 4 wickets before declaring, leaving us to score 400 to win in eight-and-a-half hours. Even with some time lost to bad light, we knew we would struggle to save the draw. In the end, we were more undone by the spin of Walters, who took four wickets, than by the pace of Lillee and Thomson, who took two apiece. Australia won the match by 171 runs, and so the series.

The record books show that we lost the fifth Test at Adelaide by 163 runs, but my memories of it are limited. Mike Denness came back into the side and I was pleased to see him hit a 50, and Derek Underwood bowled beautifully to take 11 wickets in the match. As a consolation, we even won the sixth Test back at Melbourne by an innings and four runs but, by then, my Test career was sadly over.

Fortunately, it was not all cricket on this tour. The whisky firm Famous Grouse had chosen to give samples of its excellent product to players in hopeful exchange for our attendance at a very limited number of functions. As Derek and I went to several of these, we began to build up quite a collection. We also thought it only fair to collect bottles on behalf of players too lazy to turn up. Unfortunately, our captain Mike Denness was a Scot with a serious enthusiasm for whisky, and he was determined to have his share. At one point, he came into our hotel room demanding some Famous Grouse. I insisted we had no bottles but the captain was more tenacious than I thought. He undertook a simple search and realised I was lying through my teeth. He took several bottles away, no doubt for analysis. So there can be more advantages to being captain than are first apparent.

Mike Denness spoke out boldly as the tour ended against the sub-standard umpires in Australia and New Zealand. It was not the most tactful or diplomatic speech ever made, but Mike is an honest man and, as we prepared to fly home, he said, 'In England, visiting players grumble that we give people out. In New Zealand and Australia, we find they do not give people out. Bowlers work hard for leg-before-wicket dismissals. People like Fred Titmus are very disappointed. He is not like the usual off-spinner; he can spin the ball. In Australia, he would pitch it on the line of the wicket, the sweep would be attempted but the batsmen were given not out. His art was being thrown out of the window.'

I was surprised when Mike went public, but I believe he was speaking the truth. Cricket is a game with laws that should be either obeyed or changed. While it is in force, the leg-before-wicket law should by used properly. I would certainly have taken more wickets on tour if it had been, and so would several other bowlers.

11

RINGING THE
CHANGES

Back in England, after the Australia tour, we were invited to a dinner at Number 10 by Prime Minister Harold Wilson. It was a very grand affair and I remember at one point Marcia Falkender whispering in Mr Wilson's ear and then rushing away. Some time went by, while I chatted to a couple of private secretaries who were big cricket fans. Then, suddenly, there was much confusion and consternation as a few people came in. 'What on earth does that woman think she is doing?' said one of them. 'Doesn't she know this is the Prime Minister of Great Britain, not the Mafia?' They were looking behind me, so I turned round to see Harold Wilson cheerfully chatting to Frank Sinatra. This was at a time when the singer's links with the Mafia were well known and several aides were absolutely seething that Marcia had brought him in to

Number 10; Steph and I were personally delighted to be introduced to the great singer.

After all the excitement of Australia, it was back to headquarters for the 1975 season. It wasn't a great year for Middlesex in the Championship, but we reached the finals of both the Gillette and the Benson and Hedges Cup before, unfortunately, missing out in both. I was sad to see John Murray decide to call it a day. He passed Herbert Strudwick's two world records in his final year and finished with 1,270 catches and 1,527 dismissals altogether. John had played for Middlesex for 24 seasons and we had been close all that time. I knew then I was going to miss not just his invaluable advice but also his companionship. You get to know what a bloke is like if you play serious sport with him and John is one of the best. I still managed to take 57 wickets, which was more than most, and I tried not to think too hard about the day when I would have to retire.

John had not quite started playing for Middlesex when they had had their share of the Championship in 1949 and, as soon as he left, he missed the opportunity as we won it again. For years afterwards, I used to tease him that he had been the only thing standing in our way of winning. But, in truth, 1976 was just one of those years when everything seemed to go right. It was a long, hot summer that provided great conditions for spinners, and my new partner Phil Edmonds and I had a field day. I took 65 wickets at 21.66 and Phil took 64 at 25.57. We beat Nottinghamshire by four wickets at Lord's on 27 July, taking us to the top of the table, and that's where we stayed.

In August, we had a great win over Derbyshire. I had a wonderful start with 3 wickets in the first 20 balls I bowled. Phil Sharpe was caught at deep mid-wicket and then I beat Eddie Barlow in the air and had him stumped, and then had Alan Hill caught. John Murray's former deputy, the amateur Mike Sturt, was drafted in to help out, and did a marvellous job. I finished with 12 wickets in the match for 135 and we won the game by 16 runs. We even slipped in a morale-boosting victory over the West Indians.

We won the title on 2 September at The Oval and a streaker ran on to the pitch wearing brown boots and carrying a bottle, but I waited for a drink until the champagne was cracked open later. I had played for Middlesex before three of the side were born, but that didn't bother me in the slightest. It was great to be part of a champion side and skipper Mike Brearley was widely quoted in the press as saying I had bowled marvellously. He said, 'Fred Titmus is the sort of bloke who, once he gets his teeth into something, will not let it go.' It made me sound a little like a cricketing Rottweiler, but I thought he must have meant well.

Unfortunately, that was not quite the language that Mike Brearley had used earlier that year when I tried to renegotiate my contract. I was coaching in South Africa at the time, having not been out there for 11 years. It was a great opportunity to meet some old friends and to show Stephanie and Tandy a beautiful country that I had always loved but which they had never visited before. We were based at Schoonman Park, a railway cricket club in Bloomfontein. I wrote to Middlesex to see if they would extend my current contract by a further season in order that I could return to Bloomfontein for the coming winter and at least have my job at Middlesex to return to. I was simply looking for a little security for my family and perhaps, foolishly, I thought it was a fairly straightforward request.

The reply from my captain took my breath away. Mike Brearley wrote me two long and deeply upsetting letters which spoke of my 'fading drive and ambition', telling me, 'I felt your withdrawal and bitterness was a real difficulty for the team.' The letters went on at some length and seemed to conclude that, if I bucked my ideas up and behaved myself, he might want me to stay.

I was so shocked and angry that, for the first time in a long time, I was speechless. I felt Mike's criticisms were incorrect and totally unfair. Tell me I'm too old, if that's your opinion. Tell me you think I'm past it, if that is what you think. But don't tell me my attitude is wrong, because it is precisely the same attitude which has carried me through 53 Test matches and gained me more than 20,000 runs and 2,830 wickets. I felt the same about cricket in my 40s as I did as a teenager. I loved the game and I played it to win.

When I was a young player at Lord's, the senior pros

were always treated with respect. It was an unspoken rule at Middlesex and, for me, it was what helped to make the world of cricket a decent and fulfilling arena in which to spend your working life.

For the first time, I seriously considered leaving Middlesex. I had received an offer from Tony Greig, then captain of Sussex, who said they would be delighted to have me. Maybe the time had come to move on. We were staying deep in the Orange Free State at the time and communications were not what they could have been. I felt very out of touch with the feelings of the Middlesex hierarchy. But then when George Mann, the president of the club, got to hear what was going on, he immediately cabled me in confidence, asking me not to do anything rash, and he arranged to telephone me two days later. He told me that, of course, I could extend my contract and could have carte blanche as to what I needed. He said that, after almost 27 years of service, to Middlesex I was fully entitled to that. He made me feel a whole lot better than I had for the previous few worrying weeks.

On a happier note, my cricket that winter in South Africa had gone really well. I was chosen to represent Orange Free State in the Curry Cup and we went on to win it. I also played several games for Derrick Robins XI out there. Derrick was a cricket-loving businessman who took good cricketing sides out to South Africa at a time when they were banned from international matches.

Back at Middlesex, the damning opinions of my attitude

from Mike Brearley hardly helped our relationship. When I was captain, I tried to help and encourage Mike. When he was my captain, I thought his arrogant attitude made him become something of a joke. Phil Edmonds dealt with it best. He is a very tall chap and, if Mike became heated, he would look down on him from his great height and pat him on the head and say, 'Keep your cool, Michael. Don't lose your rag.'

Brearley would fume, 'Don't pat me on the head,' as we all stood around trying not to laugh at his humiliation. Mike Brearley went on to write a book called *The Art of Captaincy*. Somehow, I've never quite found time to read it.

Philippe was also at the centre of a quite different amusing occasion at Buckingham Palace. After winning the Championship, we were to be presented with the cup at Buckingham Palace by no less than HRH the Duke of Edinburgh, who was the county's patron. We duly presented ourselves late one afternoon as directed, and we were told to await HRH's arrival. We were his fourth engagement of the day and we were just having drinks and taking photographs when Edmonds dashed in a little late and hurried to join in the photocall.

'F**k off, Phil, we don't want you in the photo,' chorused the lads.

'Oh, sorry, chaps,' replied Prince Philip, as he arrived totally unnoticed. 'I didn't mean to intrude.' Red faces all round!

There were not quite so many laughs on the field in

those days. Brearley had a way of looking good in the field, but the fact was he had a pretty good side, even when he played for England. Good captains have got to have good sides. He was not quite good enough to be a Test player.

I did push for Mike Brearley to be captain of Middlesex, but I came to regret it. As a captain, there were several occasions when we argued over Mike trying to tell me where to set my field. If he wanted to be at forward short-leg and I didn't want him there, I would pitch it up and, as soon as he had a ball whistling past his ear, he would turn and say, 'Got your point.'

The older players were not largely big fans of Brearley. When we were coming up, we were very respectful towards Denis Compton and Bill Edrich and the other senior players who had given Middlesex service for a number of years. I don't think Mike treated us in the same way when he was coming up. I certainly feel that Brearley hurried the departure of nearly all of our senior pros. He just came in and instantly wanted his own way.

Phil Edmonds arrived from Cambridge very full of himself and he also rubbed a lot of people up the wrong way. After Tony Lock, he was the best left-hand spinner around and he could bat, but he could be awkward. Brearley and Edmonds often fell out. Brearley had a very haughty manner and he was not a very good batsman – his average was about the same as mine – and he couldn't bowl. He took us back to the old days of amateurs being in charge.

If Mike Brearley had simply said he did not think I was worth another contract, I would have dealt with it and moved on. But to have my loyalty and enthusiasm questioned, and to be given advice as to my future behaviour, after almost 30 years with the county, was a bit rich. As it was, we declared an uneasy truce and won the Championship.

Unknown to me at the time, this was to be my final season with Middlesex. Winning the Championship was the icing on the cake. Two months later, I was offered the job of Surrey coach at The Oval with a contract that offered some security and a role that promised an exciting new challenge. It was the end of an era, but the start of a new one.

As things turned out, I stayed for two years of a three-year contract because it did not turn out as happily as I'd hoped. Some of the personnel there resisted a new broom, while others were helpful and co-operative. The side did not do very well and I felt that one or two knives were being sharpened. I had already turned down Surrey once before, but I took the job and I said it would take two or three years to restore the county fortunes. Unfortunately, there were those who expected instant success and there was open criticism in the dressing room. When success would not come, some players would not work hard enough to rectify it; they always wanted to blame someone else. It was so different from the atmosphere at Middlesex that I came to feel I did not want to be involved in it. I enjoyed working with Alf Gover, the chairman of the cricket committee, and John Edrich was a great professional. I also think that I left Micky Stewart, who was to follow me as coach, with the makings of a good side.

I was 46 years old and I certainly needed to keep earning a living. Cricket, in my day, was not the sort of sport that set you up for life. My wife Stephanie and I had taken over the post office in a Hertfordshire village called Potten End near Berkhamstead. To be perfectly honest, I was not a great help in the shop. My wife is very efficient and she ran the business like clockwork, aided by our wonderful, loyal staff. She used to call me the only postmaster who never sold a stamp! My work was largely restricted to the newspaper side, getting up at 5.00am every morning, and occasionally doing the paper deliveries if some of the paper boys or girls didn't turn up.

One cold and snowy winter morning, I remember carefully negotiating a tricky circular drive to a house way out in the country. I was on a small motorbike at the time and, suddenly, the postman came screaming in from the opposite direction and knocked me flying. He was going much too fast in the icy conditions. I struggled to get up, still cursing, and I knew I had injured my foot. I removed my boot and sock and held my foot up to see the damage. The blood drained from the face of the postman as he realised I had a gap where my four toes should be. He couldn't believe his eyes. Had he really managed to remove the toes from my foot just like that? He was, of course, much too young to remember the grisly details of my accident. My foot was not really badly hurt and I had to admit that he was not responsible for my lack of toes. He seemed very relieved to learn the truth.

When I was coaching Surrey, I found myself in a bizarre position. I thought I had seen and heard just about everything in cricket until, one day, I had Geoffrey Boycott crying down the phone like a baby. The ultimate Yorkshireman had a great reputation for toughness, so I was surprised and not at all sure how to react. It happened after Tony Greig was banned by the cricket authorities for accusing Boycott of ducking out of Test cricket to dodge facing up to fast bowlers like Lillee and Thomson. Greig was disciplined and I felt it was unfair, so I said so in print. I believe Greig was only banned because he was then seen as the leader of the great Kerry Packer defection which swept the game soon after I retired from Middlesex. I thought that was a completely different issue and that what Tony had said about Boycott hiding from the quick bowlers was absolutely true.

There was some publicity about my support for Tony Greig and I got lots of calls from fellow cricketers who agreed with my view. I thought the Test and County Cricket Board was quite wrong. I didn't agree with what Tony had done on behalf of Packer, but that was not what they banned him for. Tony Greig was banned for saying what most top players in England, and a number of selectors had been saying, that Geoff Boycott dropped out of the England team for three years because he did not fancy the fast bowling. I knew because I was involved.

I was on Mike Denness's tour of Australia in 1974–75 when Lillee and Thomson were knocking us all over the place. I certainly knew which selectors were muttering with complaints that Boycott was not there, after he had been originally chosen for the tour, and I know the players who felt the same way. Yet those same selectors let Boycott back into the England team within a few weeks of him deciding he would like to play again. I know Geoff Boycott did not like playing under Mike Denness, but there will always be people you don't get along with. There had been enough of them in my time.

I spoke out in April 1978. Until then, my contract as a player had forbidden me to comment. At the time, I thought my playing days were definitely over and that Tony Greig deserved my support and that I was free to say what I liked. My opinion has not changed since then. Greig was unfairly treated and Boycott should never have been allowed to play for England again. Boycott was made to look like a wounded martyr, but I have always felt what he did in quitting Test cricket was just as bad as the players who left to join Kerry Packer.

I got a lot of flak for supporting Tony Greig, but I've never regretted it. I was surprised a day or so later when Geoffrey rang me up, obviously very wound up about my comments. 'I thought you were my friend, Fred,' he said and he seemed very agitated. He spoke in a strange way, even for Geoffrey, about all the publicity and, gradually, I suspected he might have had a lawyer listening on the line, hoping I would say something incriminating that he could take action upon. I asked him about this and he seemed taken aback and he changed completely. He began to become really upset about suggestions that he was not brave enough to face the fastest of bowlers and started protesting about his reputation. To my total astonishment, he went on to break down completely. I couldn't believe what I was hearing. I told him to pull himself together. The call ended and I realised I did not understand Geoffrey Boycott at all.

My own cricket career did not end quite as finally as I thought. I was asked back to play several more games for Middlesex. I played twice in 1979, and in 1980 I was called up again. It was nice to feel wanted. The last time came when I was approaching 50 in August 1982. I just dropped in to Lord's for a chat and a cup of tea and found myself drafted into the team to play Surrey. 'Ah, Fred, you're just the man we want,' said the very same Mike Brearley, fully two years since I'd last turned out. 'The wicket is a bit loose and an extra spinner could be useful,' he added.

I had no kit with me because I was really only in London to collect an American visa from the embassy in Grosvenor Square, as I was joining an MCC tour captained by Tony Lewis to America. But Clive Radley lent me some trousers and Brearley, who was by then approaching retirement himself, provided boots and socks. A helmet was also duly produced, something I had never worn in my whole career. When I tried to refuse it, they absolutely insisted I put it on. In my early days, as you didn't have anything to protect your head, you learned pretty fast how to keep it away from the ball.

I very much enjoyed bowling alongside Phil Edmonds and John Emburey, the spinners who succeeded me, and I even managed to take 3 wickets in the second innings for 42. It was great to be able to say that I played in five decades and I was pleased to finish on friendly terms with Mike Brearley. I think I have played more games for Middlesex than anyone else, and people tell me I played more first-class cricket than anyone else since the Second World War. I don't know about that, but I do know that no one ever enjoyed playing cricket more than I did. It's a wonderful English game that inspires the sort of comradeship that lasts for lifetimes.

1 2

OVER AND OUT

Having finished playing, I served some time as a selector, which kept me in touch with the game, got me in a few too many headlines for comfort, and was not nearly so much fun as playing. Diplomacy has never been my strong point and, sometimes, an honest opinion is the last thing people really want to hear. When I went up to a match at Headingley, I was button-holed by a Geoff Boycott fan who was convinced that bringing back his favourite player was the answer to all our problems. 'Possibly,' I told him, 'but unfortunately we don't have any ten-day Test matches.' He seemed quite offended.

I think I may very well have been one of the targets in the firing line of Ian Botham, when he described the selectors as 'gin-slinging dodderers'. Ian was serving a two-month ban after admitting smoking cannabis, when he joked after a Manchester dinner how selectors are themselves chosen. Reportedly, Ian said, 'They bring him out of the loft, take the dust sheet off, give him a pink gin and then sit him there. He can't go out of a 30-mile radius of London because he's usually too pissed to get back.' Many people took this as a reference to myself, as I had just unfortunately been caught drink-driving.

I didn't take enormous exception because I never imagined anyone would believe anything Ian Botham said. He had some wonderful performances for England and he was clearly a very gifted cricketer; as a person, I was not quite so impressed. Chairman of the selectors, Peter May, said it was absolutely ridiculous, and that 'England selectors are not drunks'. I couldn't have agreed more. In any case, I have never liked gin.

My ability to hit headlines was starting to equal my record at hitting wickets because I was never frightened to speak my mind. The way cricket was run frequently left a great deal to be desired in my book. In 1989, I was astonished that a new plan was suddenly unveiled for Ted Dexter to take over from team manager Mickey Stewart and become England's new cricketing supremo. I have nothing against Ted, but I thought the way the authorities had gone about this drastic reorganisation was ridiculous… and I said so. I didn't think Ted was the man for the job because Mickey Stewart was a great professional who, in my view, was already doing a good job. What really annoyed me was everyone assuming that

Ted had been handed the job when the 17 counties had not even met to consider the plan.

David Gower was a good cricketer but not, I felt, a very good captain. His field placings were very poor. I don't think his relationship with chairman of the selectors Peter May ever recovered from the time Peter parked his car by the fire escape and caught David Gower coming down. Then there was an important meeting where David swanned in late in a very casual manner and then sat back and put his feet on the table and Peter May was not impressed. I think he would have liked to knock him into the middle of next week.

Life as a selector did have its rewarding moments and I did enjoy the contact with cricketers very much. But the politics of the game depressed and bored me. I have never been interested in scoring points over others. I would prefer to just give my opinion and get on with the job. I stuck at the selector's job until 1996, when I decided I had had enough.

Unfortunately, some people who became England captain were not, in my view, good enough and there – one who springs to mind was Mike Atherton. He was very critical of my role and that of Brian Bolus in selectors' meetings. But I was not so impressed by his behaviour, particularly when it looked to me as though he had dirt in his pockets to rub on the ball. I don't think that is the way for an England captain to behave and I don't think he was ever up to the job. Mike Atherton was not the greatest captain we ever had. He was a fair player, but he was not a good leader, and he used to turn up to lead England unshaven. The former footballer Bruce Rioch, who subsequently became a manager, is a friend of mine, and he told me he had players who turned up in that condition. He used to present them with a razor and a club fine, and I think Bruce was spot on.

The trouble was that, at the time, that there were no other obvious candidates. It was a travesty when Mike Atherton beat Peter May's record as a captain; I don't think he was fit to lace Peter May's boots.

Today, I am left with so many marvellous memories of the game. I played with some great players and some not so great players. My two great friends, John Murray and Peter Parfitt, are friends to this day, so I guess we have each other for life now. When I think back, and allow the memories to wash over me, so many players, grounds, friendships and rivalries are vividly recalled.

I am often asked to name my favourite cricketers and I always answer that it takes all sorts. The greatest opponents were always the Australians, but in every series we seemed to make far more friends than enemies. Richie Benaud is a lovely chap, a great cricketer, very down to earth and a nice guy. Most of them were. Bill Lawry was not pleasant to watch, but he was very pleasant to get out; Bobbie Simpson was a very fine player; Norman O'Neill was flashing, but could be a very fine player; Ian Chappell was a tough nut and an easy man to dislike, but he was a very fine cricketer; Brian Booth was a fine cricketer and such a nice chap he should have been an Englishman!

It was a pleasure to play at Slasher Mackay, because you knew he wasn't going to whack you round the ground. But getting him out was difficult. He was not as dour as he liked to pretend, and he did his job.

It was a different match playing Australia. Moving around the country, you met them more and the batting side would go into the other dressing room; even if there had been some heated moments on the field it was all quickly forgotten. They had a tougher attitude than anyone else we played against. Lillee and Thomson at Perth, if it pitched far in front of you, it was going to go over the top. There was a lot of bounce. It was quick but it was true so you knew what was going to happen. I was going to play back regardless. They were fearsomely quick. Thommo was the quicker of the two but, in my view, Lillee was the better bowler. In their day, I believe Trueman and Statham were just as good and they could be extremely quick as well.

In those days, we always used to be in each other's dressing rooms having a drink. When we were playing Yorkshire, we used to have to kick Trueman out of our dressing room. I think that is how sport ought to be played – hard and competitive, but with respect for the opposing team. I'm not sure that always happens nowadays, when so much money depends on the game.

As a wicket-keeper, Jim Parks was a good stopper but

he was a fine batsman. When he came into the England side, it was primarily for his batting. I didn't have the same rapport with Jim as I had with John Murray, but Jim and I did become great friends.

Of all the county sides, I always felt Yorkshire was a team full of know-alls who insisted they really knew their cricket when they didn't really know any more than anyone else. But they were one of the best sides for years, with many of the best players. There was always a different atmosphere against Yorkshire than for any other game. The crowd were more competitive and there was always a lot of edge between the sides. I always wanted to play there, even if it was sometimes a difficult experience. There was always a great rivalry up there; they simply don't like southern sides winning. Denis Compton and Bill Edrich always encouraged us to save a good performance for our visits to Yorkshire to stick it up Len Hutton and shut up the Headingley crowd. Most crowds go to watch cricket, but at Headingley they go to watch Yorkshire.

Yorkshire also seemed to breed unique cricketers who played the game in unusual ways. We were in a match against Yorkshire at the Scarborough Festival when Len Hutton was batting so slowly that Norman Yardley came in and deliberately ran him out. Norman, who was a nice guy, called out 'Yes', and then just stood there and didn't move. Len ran down and was out. Only Yorkshiremen could have treated each other like that.

Len Hutton, it goes without saying, was a legend. I was

in awe of him as a young man and I remember asking him about facing quick bowlers. 'Did you ever hook Ray Lindwall and Keith Miller, Len?' I asked.

'No, no,' he said. 'I thought about it when we were playing at Melbourne. But there is a big hospital near the ground and, when I looked up, I could see that hospital up there and I thought better of it. I didn't want to end up in there.'

I almost got my own back on my Yorkshire rivals when my youngest child was born in Leeds; had Tandy not been a girl, I would have liked the idea of a Titmus playing for Yorkshire.

Of course, Freddie Trueman and I always took the Middlesex v Yorkshire games very seriously. Off the field, we were mates and we still are. Freddie was never quite as accurate as Brian Statham, but he did so much more with the ball and he was probably quicker at times. If Fred decided he was going to have a go at you, then you had better watch out. He was also a very good short-leg and he could bat. He could get runs when he wanted to. Fred was a good companion to have on the field.

Trueman and Statham were not rivals; they complemented each other brilliantly. Fred was a swing bowler and Brian was a quick seam bowler. The difference was if Brian wanted to hit you, he hit you. With Fred, the ball came higher and you had a chance to dodge. They were a great pair and as different as chalk and cheese.

Keith Miller was a wonderful player but he never got on

too well with Don Bradman. The last time I saw Keith, in 2002, we were watching a match at Lord's and he was in his wheelchair. He reached over and grabbed me in a grip that felt like a vice and said, 'That bloody Bradman. He was a bastard.'

I said, 'You seemed to do all right with him.'

Keith said, 'Oh yes, he was a good cricketer, but that doesn't stop from being a bloody bastard.'

Keith was pretty wild on and off the field and I think there was a major personality clash there somewhere. He went on about Bradman for about 20 minutes and he was really having a go but, at the end of it all, he did admit that Bradman had been a really good player.

Ray Illingworth – I was in the RAF with him, and we've been friends ever since. He was a very good player who became my main rival for a Test place for years. I never minded being replaced by Ray, so long as it didn't happen too often. Raymond and I had the same ideas and same feelings about the game.

David Allen and I were good friends as well as rivals. He was on the first Australian tour. We accepted whatever decision was made, and got on with it. It was the same with Raymond Illingworth; he started off bowling seamers and then went on to bowl off-spinners just as I did. We all had our time. Raymond was a very good cricketer but he is not exactly a barrel of laughs. He had a Yorkshire sense of humour. It was in there somewhere, but you had to look hard for it.

When I think of Pat Pocock, I can't help remembering a Middlesex v Surrey match at Lord's. Pat – known as Percy – was an off-spinner, and came in at number eight wearing a pair of glasses. I usually bowled from the Pavilion End because the slope from the Grandstand down to the Tavern helped my spin. I saw Percy approaching and couldn't resist asking, 'Come on, Perce. It can't be that bad. What are you wearing the bins (glasses) for?'

Percy tried to ignore the teasing but, as he got level, he said quite abruptly, 'So I can hear you better, of course,' and he proceeded to take guard.

I'll never forget what happened next – I got him first ball. It went straight through between bat and pad and hit the top of the middle stump. Percy began the long walk back looking particularly glum and, as he passed me, I couldn't resist, 'You didn't hear that too well, Percy!'

Another character I remember well is Roy Swetman. We were good pals because we had been on the infamous Pakistan tour of 1956 when the umpire Idris Begh was soaked. He came in to bat at Surrey. There was always plenty of banter between myself and 'Swety' and, one day, he came in to bat at Lord's and, as he passed me, I cheekily said, 'Roy, do you mind getting me a glass of water on your way back?' Roy responded fairly aggressively to this jibe, as you might expect, but three balls later he was on his way back. I couldn't resist saying, 'Don't forget to bring the water, Roy.'

In the early days, we had big old leather bags to carry

all our gear around. They were extremely heavy and we used to accumulate no end of stuff in these bags; I'm afraid to say we only used to empty them once or twice a year. At Lord's one day, some joker (I suspect it was Parfitt or Murray) slipped a triangle of Camembert into my bag. It went all the way to South Africa for five months and back home again. When I opened up my bag next season, they all said, 'What the hell is that smell?' Eventually, we found the cheese in the very bottom of my bag and everyone had a go at me for not looking after my things more carefully.

Whenever we had free days, they were often spent on the golf course and the competition between us was always intense. I beat Parfitt one day and won a ball. He presented me with what looked like a brand-new Dunlop 65, only he had just used the famous crinkly paper to wrap up a very old, very badly cut ball. He even carefully glued the label down. He tossed it to me and said, 'I'll have that back the next time we play.' It was all a bit too easy and I knew something was wrong, so I told Peter I did not trust him. I unwrapped it straight away and the dressing room erupted.

Of all the memorable umpires I have come across, Arthur Fagg from Kent is one man who always brings a smile when I think of him. We were playing Surrey at The Oval, but John Murray had an injured finger and could not play. He walked through the Long Room at The Oval and Godfrey Evans was doing the odds on various things and one of the items you could bet on was batsmen getting 100. Eric Russell, who opened the batting for Middlesex, was 10-1. Mike Smith, the other opener, was 12-1, as was Clive Radley. Peter Parfitt was down at 16-1. As Peter had been the leading Middlesex batsman for ten years, John Murray did not waste any opportunity to tease him in the changing room. 'Obviously, Godfrey thinks you can't play, Parf,' said John.

Parfitt had a look at the wicket and pronounced it a 'shirt-front' that he backed himself to get 100 on. He took a fiver out of his pocket and gave it to JT and said, 'You just put that on my nose.' He was not known as a betting man and that inspired a lot of people to have a bet on him as well.

John Murray, because he wasn't playing, was able to bet and he went and put the money on. Parfitt eventually went in before lunch and at tea he was 70-odd not out. This was towards the end of the season with neither side in with any chance of the Championship, so there were only two men and a dog in the ground. When Parf was on 97, he was at he non-striker's end. Arthur Fagg said to him, 'How much have you got on it?'

Parf denied all knowledge, naturally, and insisted he was not allowed to bet.

With that, Arthur Fagg took a ticket out of his top pocket and said, 'Well, I wouldn't bother too much about it if I were you!'

Eventually, Parf hit Graham Roope through the covers to get 100 and the whole Middlesex balcony roared with approval. They just took off. Dear old Alex Bannister was just about the only press man there and couldn't understand why Parf was doing a football-style celebration in the middle.

Frank Lee was an interesting umpire. I was bowling in Portsmouth and, at the end of the over, he said to me quietly, 'You don't want that fielder there, Fred, you want him over there.' So I took his advice moved the fielder and, only a few balls later, he got a catch. So it definitely used to pay to keep on the right side of the umpires.

I was bowling at umpire Eddie Philipson's end, and I had had one or two appeals ruled not out and became a bit disillusioned. Then I went round the wicket and the batsman went forward and it was a sort of marginal decision, so I thought there was no point in appealing and turned round and saw Eddie gesticulating at me, and so I appealed and the umpire went, 'That's out.' It must have been the longest delayed appeal ever, but it took the wicket.

The foreign teams did not walk. I think the reason is that their umpires were not as good as our umpires. There is a history of poor decisions and, when you have been given out wrongly a few times, then you're not inclined to walk when you think you might get the rub of the green on another day. Here, though, when Bill Edrich was captain, you were in trouble if you didn't walk when you were out. You got a bollocking, and Bill didn't mince words. 'Why didn't you walk?' he would ask.

'Well, I … er …'

'Well, you bloody well walk in future. Their job is hard enough as it is.'

Of course, it is a sportsmanship thing as well, but that seems to have gone nowadays.

In my opinion, there were better umpires about than Dickie Bird, but he was quite good and he was a character. Dickie was entertaining with all his twitching and marching about.

There were no umpires I dreaded; not, at least, when I was captain, because I had to mark them. Generally speaking, when you're writing the report, you would mention the umpire. We never tried to mark anybody down.

I would say our worst umpire was as good as the Australians' best umpire or the South Africans' best umpire. Most of ours were ex-players, while a lot of other countries seemed to recruit them from all over the place.

If I think of the great sportsmen I've been privileged to play with, Denis Compton must rank up there with the best of them. He played in the Cup Final and, at half-time, the manager Tom Whittaker told Denis to make the most of it because 'this is the last game of football you're going to play'. Of course, Denis went out in the second-half and played a blinder. After that, he carried on playing cricket, where you could get away with having a bad knee at cricket – just. But I always wondered just how good he would have been if he hadn't had the bad knee.

Denis was the one genius of the game I had the honour

of playing with. He made his own rules and he was very good to bat with; he was very generous. If there was someone a bit quick at one end, he would say to you, 'I'll stay up here and sink this bloke.' He was a terrific player. He played shots which were so brilliant they defied belief. He could defend as well as anyone else, but when he was attacking he was extraordinary. You simply couldn't set a field to contain him, let alone stop him.

All the players would come on the balcony to watch him. We had a shove ha'penny board in the dressing room, and Bill Edrich and Denis were both very good at it, but nobody played shove ha'penny when Denis was batting.

When I joined Middlesex, I got to bat with my hero and I had to pinch myself to make sure I wasn't dreaming. I used to stand at the non-striker's end and watch him batting and think to myself, 'You can't do that.' But he could do it and he kept doing it. He was a bit of a nuisance in the field because he kept wandering about. You would ask him to field somewhere and that's where he would start off, but he fielded where he wanted to field. If he thought he might have a better chance of getting a catch 30 yards away, then that is where he would go. So, if you finally got a batsman to hit a ball in his direction, it was deeply frustrating to look over and see that he was no longer there.

Denis was not always easy. He could be a nightmare to bat with because his running between the wickets was often erratic. He would call 'Yes' and then change his mind without telling you, and you wouldn't realise what was going on until you were stranded halfway down the wicket... and you had to run back and be out. You knew you could never run Denis out. Our captain, Walter Robins, made it quite clear that if you ran Denis out, then your chances of selection for the next fixture were seriously impaired. You had to sacrifice yourself.

As for the heroes of today, Andrew Flintoff is a modern-day Botham. I looked up his record before the most recent series and it wasn't that good. Botham was not the most liked person, but perhaps you need a bit of arrogance. As a selector, I picked him and I played against him. He was on his way up and I was on my way out. To me, the records speak volumes. Flintoff is full of potential but he still has something to prove.

I only played under Brian Close a couple of times, but I always felt he was the best captain I played for. He was not the greatest player, but he was an inspirational sort of guy. He started as a batsman who could bowl off spinners and seamers. He didn't bowl a lot, but he could do it, so he understood what sort of field you wanted. With Brian, you always felt as if you were working together. I think Brian knew more about the game than any other captain I played under. He was a hard man and I think he should have captained England more often than he did. He was certainly better than Cowdrey and Dexter.

And it was Ted Dexter who usually wanted bowlers to bowl to the field he set, which was sometimes unhelpful to a bowler. Ted was a great player, but he was also a hard man and he wanted the best out of you, so he could get a little angry sometimes. One day at The Oval, I bowled all afternoon and went for about 20 runs in 20 overs. Ted had earlier said to me, 'Try to keep the scoring down if you can.' He came out after tea and I said, 'I'll have the same field.'

Ted flipped. He said, 'You've been bowling bloomin' defensive all day. Now attack!'

Mike Smith would never do that. He would have a chat with you and suggest things and you would come to a joint decision. Ted's idea of a joint decision was him telling you what to do and you doing it. He was a prickly character.

Even Colin Cowdrey sometimes liked to direct you and be in charge. That always upsets a bowler. He was a posh chap, who'd been to public school and to university, so he was much more sophisticated than the likes of me. Colin was a great player – he was an excellent first slip – but he was not a very good captain. He used to be at first slip when I was bowling, and if I wanted something changing in the field, I used to find he was a long way away from me. Colin didn't want you to move fielders; he wanted the field as he wanted it, and that was final. So you would find yourself bowling balls you didn't want to bowl and it was inhibiting at times. It doesn't sound very significant, but it makes a huge difference to your effectiveness as a bowler. Colin, though, to give him his due, was more skilled at handling bowlers when the time had come for a change. He would take you off with a kind word and a suggestion that you might have a beer later, while Ted would just say, 'You've had enough now. Get down to third man.'

I was around when Colin Cowdrey's son was selected for the England team. It shouldn't have happened because he wasn't good enough. Richard Hutton was a similar case; he was a good cricketer but, in my opinion, he was not an England cricketer.

Warwickshire's Mike Smith was also a very fine captain, close in ability to Brian Close. Mike accepted that if you were a Test bowler, you probably knew where you wanted your field setting and he would leave you to it. If you were bowling reasonably well, he would leave you to get on with it. If you're playing for England, you shouldn't need to be told how to bowl. Colin sometimes chipped in, and Ted was often very forceful and direct, but Mike just let you bowl and went to stand at short-leg. You have to be a brave man to stand at short-leg, and I had to be careful to make sure he didn't get a whack.

If I cast my mind back to some of the other greats I played with, Freddie Trueman looms large in the memory. I had quite a few stands with Freddie because, often for England, I would be in at number eight and Freddie would follow at number ten. Freddie was always a much better batsman than he was given credit for. He could bat as well as bowl and he had one of the best throwing arms I have ever seen. His throws were so strong and accurate he was responsible for a lot of runouts, and he would field at short-leg as well. As I mentioned earlier, he could also be quite unorthodox in his approach, particularly when he hit a six and then appealed against the light. Only Freddie could have done that.

We often bowled at opposite ends and it was frequently quite effective because we were so different in style. Batsmen who were trying to get a move on found it hard to get after both of us successfully. I used to think that Freddie got me a lot of wickets because batsmen could not get after him because he was moving the ball so much so they would try to get after me and I got them out.

Freddie and I had lots of tangles when Middlesex played Yorkshire. But whatever he did on the pitch, Freddie was always worth having in the dressing room because he always lifted everyone's spirits with his sense of humour.

Brian 'George' Statham had a wonderful action and he bowled with an accuracy and consistency that was rarely equalled by anyone I played with. Freddie was more of a swing bowler, who could really make the ball move in the air and he could send it down pretty fast if he wanted to as well. Brian was also quick, but the worst thing about playing against him was that he could make the ball nip back from outside off-stump, something that often used to result in hitting you on the inside of thigh – and it didn't half hurt. John Murray used to suffer from this particularly. George had a good sense of humour, but Fred was great… as Freddie will tell you if you ask him!

I started in the RAF with Freddie, so we were friends

from the very early days. He was always pretty outspoken and some of the young officers who tried to knock Freddie's bowling around a bit soon found balls whistling round their ears, so they treated him with a bit more respect after that. Trueman and Statham were both very good fielders, and very good company.

Freddie was a very competitive golfer as well, but you had to watch him pretty closely, if you know what I mean. Freddie is the best after-dinner speaker I have ever heard. Even if you've heard the stories before, Freddie could make you laugh all over again in the way he told them. I loved playing against Freddie because he was always very competitive and, afterwards, if you'd managed to get the better of him at all, you'd probably hear 'You lucky little bastard…' but it was always meant in fun.

John Edrich was also a good player. He was a great batsman in that he never allowed anything to upset him, least of all the previous ball. I got fed up with beating him twice an over and still having to suffer him taking eight runs off the other four balls.

Gary Sobers was another wonderful cricketer; if you ever got him out, you were pleased with yourself. I remember bowling to him at Nottingham and, before he had even got off the mark, he played and got an edge and it shot off sideways. It hit Murray, the wicket-keeper, pretty hard and bounced to Parfitt at first slip… and he dropped it. I had a go at both of them in fun. I said, 'I'm supposed to have the best wicket-keeper in the world and the best first slip in the world. What happened? We should have got the best cricketer in the world out.'

Gary Sobers was a very sociable guy, and he was always in our dressing room. That day, he came in afterwards and said, 'Titmus! Murray! Parfitt! Upstairs.' He invited us up and opened a bottle of Mount Gay Rum from his native Barbados and made it clear that none of us were to leave until the bottle was empty. We sat there for a while and it was very enjoyable. He might not have been the best batsman I ever played against, although he was close, but he was certainly the best cricketer.

For sportsmen and women to achieve success in their chosen field, the talent has got to be there at the start. There is not an awful lot you can add, but I think too much coaching can be harmful. Since I've retired, I've often been asked to help out bowlers, and there was a young Indian Test player that I was able to improve quite dramatically, but only because of a very slight adjustment. He had all the talent, but he was just doing one small thing incorrectly. His main problem was that his run up was much too long. I cut it down from 15 yards to 6, and he was instantly a much better bowler. It made him better balanced when he got to the wicket and it saved a lot of energy. I don't know why he was taking a long run up in the first place, because he was not bowling fast. Fortunately, he accepted the advice, so I got the praise but he had the talent. After that, he went back to India and started getting a lot of wickets.

People say how much fitter today's players are, but I'm

not so sure. A lot of the cricketers in my day also played football and they were pretty fit. We trained but, generally, we played such a lot of cricket that we kept fit through playing cricket six hours a day.

Ken Barrington became a great pal. He wasn't a big striker of the ball like some of the others so perhaps he didn't hit as many headlines. But he was a very fine batsman and he had a wonderful sense of humour.

We used to tease him unmercifully about his tendency to score rather slowly; he loved it and always gave as good as we got. When we played Surrey at home, and he came out to bat, one of us – me, Parfitt or Murray – would say, 'Now look, Ken. We have got a lot of people here at Lord's today and we don't want you to bore them.' And we always got an earful in return.

I once got him out at Lord's with the last ball before lunch. His face fell. As we walked in, Ken looked at me, Parfitt and Murray and said, 'That would have to happen against you lot, wouldn't it. Bastards!' We had a very jolly lunch trying to get Kenny to explain to us where exactly he had gone wrong.

Kenny also used to do all sorts of things to get a laugh. I remember him getting a tin tray from somewhere and putting coins on it and then going round the England dressing room tapping it and singing 'Land of Hope and Glory' and he would get a few followers and lead a parade round the dressing room all singing loudly together. Kenny was a great man for raising the spirits.

Once, at a dull moment in a Test in India, the crowd were getting a bit restless and he just bent down to pick the ball up but, instead of taking hold of it cleanly, he deliberately kicked it forward as he bent down. He looked baffled and then did it again. Before you knew it, 70,000 people were laughing fit to burst and the whole mood of the day had changed. Kenny was priceless.

I think it was one of the saddest days of my life when I was playing golf at Rye with the county cricketers one Sunday when the message came through that Kenny had died. He was only just into his fifties, a couple of years older than me, and we shared the same birth date. We always used to celebrate together if we could, and Kenny was one of my closest friends.

When I think back to some of the techniques used by some players to gain the upper hand in tense situations, one of the most publicised has been sledging, but in my experience, sledging was very, very rare. There was a little bit of back-chat and joking here and there, but mainly the matches were played in a sporting spirit. I don't think umpires then would have stood for this swearing and jeering that goes on on the field today. We enjoyed ourselves so much; it was a kinder era, and I think the players were just as good and, in many cases, better, if I'm honest. There was always a lot of banter but usually it was more between ourselves. Murray, Parfitt and I were always having a go at each other in a good-natured way and, as we were all a little deaf, these conversations would become something of a feature of playing at Lord's.

When we weren't pulling each other's legs, my colleagues could often give me some interesting perspectives on my bowling. John Murray, for example, could tell what I was going to bowl before I bowled it. There was the off-spinner, there was the roller, there was a little swinger and there was the quick ball. I said to him one day, 'How the bloody hell do you know what I am going to bowl when I don't always know myself?' He said it was the position of my body as I came up. If my elbow was pointing a particular way, I was going to bowl that ball, and so on. They were indicators that I hadn't been aware of. I was very impressed and greatly helped by John's brilliance behind the stumps.

While I was a selector, the possibility of playing for any nation other than England was suddenly put to me… in jest, I should add. I went up to watch Northants play against Ireland at Northampton. Ireland were batting and I was sitting close to some Irish selectors. We got talking and I happily volunteered that I was a quarter Irish, my grandmother having come from Ireland. Humour is an art form over the Irish Sea, so without even the hint of a pause, the reply flashed back, 'Can you play tomorrow?'

Of course, part of the job of being a high-profile cricketer involved participating in matches with celebrities from time to time, and I've had to bowl to some interesting characters. On one occasion, I was bowling to Prince Phillip in a charity match and, of course, I had to keep him in. Mind you, he was almost minor club standard as a cricketer, and by no means an idiot, but we had to give him a few full tosses to get him off the mark.

Elton John was not nearly as good as that. Before playing in my second benefit in 1973, he came in the dressing room needing some kit. We gave him some shoes and, when he took his own off, he disappeared. He was wearing platform soles and shrank at least five inches. He did have green hair as well, but that didn't matter too much as he threw himself into enjoying his cricket..

When thinking about how the game has changed in recent years, we used to bowl around 20 overs an hour, but now the rate seems to have gone down to 12 or 13, which is hardly value for money. At one time, I used to get told to slow down because you can easily bowl a maiden over in under three minutes if you get on with it. When I started, I used to bowl with Jack Young who was getting on a bit and he would soon call me over and tell me to slow down. But when I was told to slow down because the opposition were scoring too fast, it still only took me five minutes.

When I look back over my career, one thing was always true for me – cricket was such fun. I played until I was 46 or 47 because I enjoyed it. I suppose it's also true that I wasn't too qualified to do anything else! But I played because I enjoyed playing; wherever we went, we generally found ourselves to be among friends.

Nowadays, of course, players have agents and sponsored cars and can make a great deal of money. But from what I see of cricket, they don't have quite the same level of camaraderie and they don't get as much enjoyment out of the game as we managed. But it is still a wonderful game and I am looking forward to the visit of the Australians in the summer of 2005 as much as anyone. We have the makings of a team good enough to mount a decent challenge to the all-conquering Aussies at last, and that is very good for the game.